HERO DOGS

SECRET MISSIONS
AND SELFLESS SERVICE

WHITE STAR PUBLISHERS

CONTENTS

Preface   RONALD L. AIELLO

Text   LANCE BACON

Editorial Project   VALERIA MANFERTO DE FABIANIS

Editorial Staff   GIADA FRANCIA

Grafic Design   MARIA CUCCHI

3 *A 1917 recruiting poster.*

4-5 *"Dino" sits during a memorial service for "Dino"'s handler, Staff Sgt. Christopher Diaz.*

6-7 *A U.S. Army soldier with his military working dog jump out of a CH-47 Chinook helicopter*

8-9 *U.S. Marines run toward a UH-1 Huey helicopter in the Tay Ninh area of Vietnam.*

As we entered the clearing of the second village we were searching that day, "Stormy" my service dog went down and looked into the air to our right. I instinctively followed him down. The two bullets from the sniper's rifle zinged past my ear. The Marines behind us returned fire and there was silence. It wouldn't be the last time that my friend would save me and a good number of others in the fields and jungles of Vietnam. In fact, when you've been in combat with a Service Dog the statement that dogs are man's best friend isn't even close. A service dog is part of you and also you're guardian angel. The following pages are a fitting tribute to a side of war and some very courageous heroes that many have missed. Dogs have been in the toughest fights throughout history.

In modern warfare, the dogs and their handlers have set a new standard of performance. From sentries to scouts and on to bomb sniffing, the Service Dog Teams have become trained to the absolute maximum of performance. When you spend time with a service dog the bond is incredible, and what a dog can do with their natural instincts and senses is amazing. As General David H. Petraeus stated in 2008 as the top commander in Iraq, "The capability the Military War Dogs bring to the fight cannot be replicated by men or machines. By all measures of performance their yield outperforms any asset we have in our inventory."

Military Working Dogs and their Handlers serve in a special way with a special bond between them. Perhaps, it is fitting in this case to say that Military Working Dog Teams are definitely a different breed.

They learn new ways to communicate where actions truly do mean more than words.

They learn to work in total sync with each other for the protection and good of others.

They develop a rare relationship where both completely know the heart and soul of the other.

When they signed on for a combat mission, they acknowledged that they would not only be part of a mission, but that they were there to protect everyone on that mission in an incredible way.

These Military Working Dog Teams would willing give their all for us and for many they would never know...

In 2000, as a result of our respect for our dogs and the heroism and sacrifice of war dogs and handlers, five of us Vietnam dog handlers formed the U.S. War Dogs Association. The association is committed to promoting the long history of the Military Working Dogs, establishing permanent war dog memorials and educating the public about the invaluable service of these Military Working Dogs to our country. Over the past couple of years, we have created Operation Military Care K9 to make sure that the Military War Dog Teams deployed in the Middle East are receiving complete support. We raise funds to send care packages and letters of encouragement to the Dog Teams.

Military Working Dogs who are trained and skillfully disciplined will save countless lives during their time in the military. We will never know all of their heroic deeds and sacrifices' because of Military Secrecy.

Today's Military Working Dogs are finally receiving the recognition they deserve by the Armed Forces of the United States and our Allies of the United Nations.

These Courageous War Dogs are our first line of defense.

Ronald L. Aiello

11 Vietnam veteran Ron Aiello stands with his war dog, "Stormy". He is now president of the United States War Dog Association.

12-13 Iraq and Afghanistan have seen as many as 1,200 dog teams in action at one time. Improvised Explosive Devices are responsible for more than half of coalition troops killed. When war dogs are in the operation, the IED detection rate jumps to as high as eighty percent.

14-15 Military Working Dogs endure combat conditions right alongside their handlers. Like soliders, a prevalence of post-traumatic stress is apparent among war dogs, and, like humans, PTSD affects each war dog differently

A Timeless Loyalty.

Amid the brutal battlefields that litter human history emerges a tale rarely told. Though it speaks of courage and camaraderie, this is not the story of common men who display uncommon valor in the face of certain death. It is instead the story of four-legged fighters who stand tall as the fury of war rages all around them.

Nearly every time man has stepped into battle, a dog has served alongside. But among them stand an elite class of dogs carefully selected for special capabilities such as stamina, faithfulness and aggression.

Pharaoh Rameses II and his Egyptian Empire inaugurated the first legion when he fastened spiked collars to blood thirsty war dogs that raced ahead of his armies to score the battle's first victory. The subsequent world powers of Assyria, Babylon, Persia, Greece and Rome took the use of war dogs to new highs, and lows.

The Romans were so skilled in this arena that they were able to convert the typically gentle Mastiff into a vicious and fearless fighter. Such a reputation was matched only by the terror-inducing sight of this massive canine, wrapped in spike-covered armor and charging at full speed.

16-17 A WWI allied soldier bandages the paw of a Red Cross dog on May 5, 1917. The Red Cross dogs were renown for their ability to locate wounded soldiers otherwise lost amid brutal battlefields and trenches.

The lesson was not lost on renowned military strategists such as Attila the Hun, Alexander the Great and Hernan Cortes. Even the placid American statesman Benjamin Franklin suggested the Pennsylvania militia use attack dogs against Indian raids.

Yet the role of war dogs has not been confined to offensive aggression. Napoleon Bonaparte enlisted dogs not for their ferocity, but to detect and warn of impending attack. The American Civil War saw the rise of messenger dogs and Theodore Roosevelt used scout dogs when his famous Rough Riders patrolled Cuban jungles during the Spanish-American War.

But it was the selfless service of war dogs in World War I that truly captured the world's attentions and imagination and with good reason.

More than seventy-five thousand dogs served in World War I. The Germans started the war with six thousand dogs on the front and four thousand in reserve. Italy fielded three thousand dogs.

Marshal Joseph Joffre inexplicably shut down France's military dog program after the Battle of the Marne in 1914, but not before the nation's war dog force totaled fifteen thousand.

The British started the war with just one dog — and one visionary dog trainer. Lt. Col. E. H. Richardson, who trained and supplied ambulance dogs for the Russian army during the Russo-Japanese War of 1904 and convinced British war planners to launch a dog program. Richardson was promoted to colonel and ordered to establish the British War Dog School, which eventually provided thousands of dogs for the war effort.

Regardless of nationality, war dogs proved far less likely to get captured or shot. They were used to deliver food, messages and ammunition. But the most revered canines were the venerable "Red Cross dogs."

These canines braved the choking stench of mustard and phosgene gases to locate wounded soldiers obscured by the fog of war and otherwise

lost on the blood-stained battlefield. The soldier would find comfort in the medical supplies and water attached to the dog's harness. But the greatest comfort was in knowing the dog that quickly rushed off would soon return — leading a rescue team to the location.

The soldier in need was especially lucky if found by "Prusco," a French Red Cross dog known to first drag casualties into the cover of craters and trenches.

The dog, said to resemble a white wolf, located more than one hundred wounded men in one day alone.

The most famous dog to emerge from World War I served for a short time on the front lines, but in a very different role. "Rin Tin Tin," who was later featured in twenty-three Hollywood movies, was a five-day-old puppy when he was rescued from bombarded ruins on September 15, 1918 by American serviceman Lee Duncan in Lorraine, France.

18-19 Just like the soldiers they serve alongside, a dog's military service is not always glamorous. Some, like this Austrian Dog Transport Corps in World War I, were used to pull supply loads on small carts.

20-21 More than half a dozen "Red Cross Dogs" move to the next mission during service in World War I. Thousands of these rescue dogs were laden with medical supplies and water. They would first locate wounded soldiers then lead a rescue team back to the location.

The star of the silver screen proved to be an exception to the rule. Estimates of war dogs killed in "The Great War" range from seven thousand to sixteen thousand. Tens of thousands more were destroyed as armies demobilized. Only Germany maintained its dog program after the war. The nation graduated nearly 200,000 war dogs in the 1930s from a training school in Frankfurt and had more than 50,000 in service by the time the United States entered World War II. The Germans supplied Japan with an additional 25,000 war dogs before the Dec. 7, 1941 attack on Pearl Harbor.

The American military, which had no real war dog program during World War I, had a dismal fifty sled dogs at the time of that attack. These dogs were survivors and offspring of the team that took Rear Admiral Richard Byrd on his second Antarctic expedition from 1933 to 1935.

22-23 Like the German soldiers shown here, combatants on both sides of the battlefield developed gas masks to protect their war dogs from mustard and phosgene gases during World War I.

The immediate need for war dogs was not lost on war planners. Secretary of War Harold Stimson on July 16, 1942, gave the order to train search and rescue sled dogs, patrol dogs and messenger dogs. Initial estimates called for one-hundred twenty five thousand dogs, but far fewer would be needed.

A not-for-profit organization called "Dogs for Defense" quickly came to the rescue. It coordinated the recruitment of forty thousand dogs in only two years. Eighteen thousand dogs representing thirty-two breeds were accepted for initial training. That cadre was trimmed to ten thousand four hundred twenty-five dogs, which received advanced training at five War Dog Reception and Training Centers.

The number of breeds was simultaneously trimmed to seven. German shepherds and Doberman Pinschers were chosen for sentry, attack and scout missions. Sled-pulling Siberian Huskies, Malamutes and Eskimo dogs were selected to find air crews downed in inaccessible snow-covered areas. Collies and Belgian Sheepdogs were assigned messenger missions.

The Coast Guard also used more than eighteen hundred dogs to patrol American beaches.

While Dogs for Defense covered the Army's need, the Marine Corps turned to the Doberman Pinscher Club of America and private citizens for help. The Corps ended up with more than one thousand dogs, with Dobermans outnumbering German Shepherds three-to-one. Seven war dog platoons were fielded and trained at Camp Lejeune, N.C. and all seven would see heavy action against relentless Japanese defenses entrenched throughout the Pacific.

The First Marine War Dog Platoon braved intense mortar and heavy machinegun fire as part of the initial assault on Bougainville. It also fought on Guam and Okinawa.

24 *A German soldier in 1916 gives instruction to his messenger dog. France and Great Britain also made great use of these swift messengers, which were far less likely to be wounded or captured.*

25 *Germans on the Western front in 1918 stand guard with their trusted canine. Only Germany maintained its dog program after the Great War, and had more than 50,000 dogs in service by the time the United States entered World War II.*

The second and third war dog platoons operated in six locations. The most notable among them was Guam, where dog teams conducted more than four-hundred fifty patrols, alerted to enemy activity one-hundred seventy times and were responsible for two-hundred sixty nine enemy kills.

The seventh war dog platoon hit the volcanic sands of Iwo Jima's black beach on the amphibious assault's deadly first day. The sixth platoon later came ashore to locate hidden tunnels and pillboxes.

The fourth, fifth and sixth platoons fought on Okinawa.

26 "Mark" was an ammunition carrier given to British Expeditionary Forces by the First French Army. He saw active service in France from November 1939 to June 1940, and was part of the forces that drove north to meet the German invasion of France.

26-27 A British soldier inserts a message into the collar of a dog trained at the Army School of Dog Training in 1941. The dog was one of seven hundred being prepared for combat service.

27

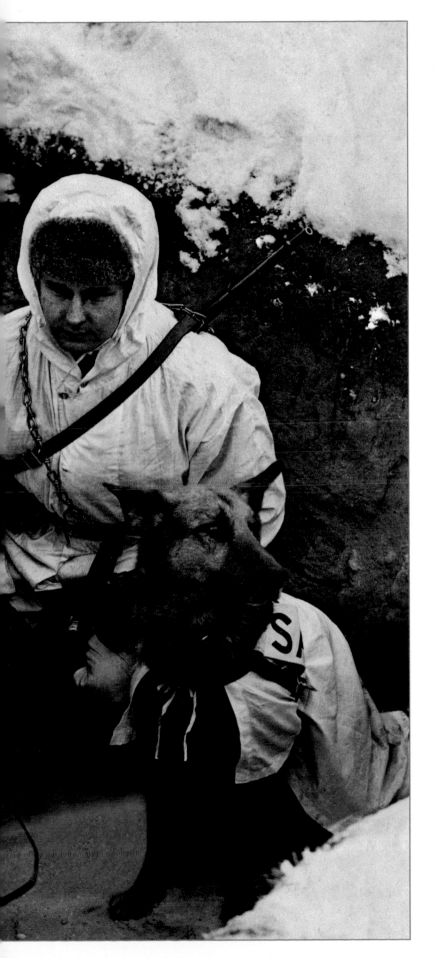

Dogs and handlers from the fifth platoon, which also landed on the second day of the Peleliu invasion, joined Marine scouts on a dangerous reconnaissance mission of Okinawa five days before that invasion. The fourth and sixth platoon later received presidential unit citations for their service on the island.

It was during the Pacific Island Hopping Campaign that dog handlers first encountered threats that proved as dangerous and deadly as any enemy soldier. More war dogs would succumb to heat-related illness and diseases than to combat for decades to come.

World War II saw a concerted effort in mine detection. Most units could not achieve a ninety-percent effective rate, the golden standard for explosive detection. The Russians reportedly had a dog that found two thousand mines in eighteen days while clearing railroad tracks and key airports. Russians also strapped bombs to dogs trained to look for food under tanks. But German tanks used a different fuel than Russian tanks, and the dogs went where they were trained to go – and blew up their own tanks in the process.

The U.S. military "retrained" its war dogs at the end of hostilities with the intent of returning them to original owners and adopted homes. Only nineteen of the five-hundred fifty nine surviving Marine dogs had to be destroyed – fifteen for health reasons and four due to behavior. Only four of the three thousand dogs discharged by the Army had to be returned.

The post-war discharge was the last of its kind. Military working dogs now remain in service until they are too old or too injured to serve.

28-29 Two Alsatian dogs train with the Finnish Army in March 1940. The letters "SA" seen on their white snow-cloaks stand for Suomen Armeija (Finnish Army).

30-31 Heat-related illness and diseases killed more war dogs in the Pacific during World War II than enemy action. That reality would only increase in Vietnam, where hundreds of dogs died from heat and disease. In the current wars, officials say that "only a handful" of dogs have died from these causes.

32-33 A U.S. Marine chats with his scouting dog on Guam in August 1944. The dogs were used to track down Japanese soldiers hidden in caves or jungle strongholds and for running messages.

33 U.S. Marine Pfc. Rez P. Hester of the 7th War Dog Platoon, 25th Regiment, takes a nap while "Butch", his war dog, stands guard. This photo was taken on Iwo Jima in February 1945. The famous flag raising on Mount Suribachi took place that same month, only a short distance away.

34-35 *The First Marine War Dog Platoon is credited with the Corps' first canine combat action of World War II when the unit landed with Marine Raiders on Bougainville Island in the Northern Solomon Islands, in November 1943.*

36 U.S. Army Sgt. William C. Dutton, assisted by Technician
Fifth Grade Marvin Monshousen, bandages the injured paw
of "Thunders" on Sept. 6, 1946. The dog was a member
of the 38th Quartermaster War Dog Platoon, 85th Division,
based in Northern Italy.

37 A U.S. Marine dog handler comforts his German Shepherd
while the dog is X-rayed after being shot by a Japanese sniper
on Bougainville. The dog died of its injuries.

Despite showing unquestionable worth in Europe and especially in the Pacific, post-war cutbacks proved devastating to the once mighty military dog platoons. Only one active scout dog platoon existed when the Korean War started – the 26th Infantry Platoon (Scout Dog) based at Fort Riley, Kansas. It consisted of a commanding officer, platoon sergeant, veterinarian, eighteen dog handlers and twenty-seven dogs.

And it was about to be put to the test.

The 26th Infantry Platoon (Scout Dog) was ordered to Korea in May 1951, and arrived one month later as military leaders scrambled to find suitable dogs to fill the ranks.

Though attached to the Second Infantry Division, the platoon never received the equipment it needed to care for, let alone operate with its dogs. But that did not stop the dogs or their handlers from performing above and beyond the call of duty. The platoon would complete its tour of duty on January 15, 1953, having earned three Silver Stars, six Bronze Stars with Valor device and thirty-five Bronze Stars for meritorious service.

The Department of the Army in General Orders No. 21 said the platoon's "unbroken record of faithful and gallant performance of these missions by individual handlers and their dogs in support of patrols have saved countless casualties through giving early warning to the friendly patrol of threats to its security." General Orders No. 114, issued by Eighth United States Army, said that "throughout its long period of difficult and hazardous service, the 26th Infantry Scout Dog Platoon has never failed those with whom it served; has consistently shown outstanding devotion to duty in the performance of all of its other duties, and has won on the battlefield a degree of respect and admiration which has established it as a unit of the greatest importance to the Eighth United States Army."

The Army ultimately used about fifteen hundred war dogs in Korea. Open territories forced patrols to operate at night. Pentagon statistics show patrols that utilized scout dogs saw sixty percent fewer casualties. Dogs also guarded air bases and fuel and ammunition depots.

Despite the meritorious, even heroic service displayed over the previous fifteen years, the Army and Marines no longer saw a great need for war dogs.

The Air Force saw things differently.

The service needed sentry dogs to guard nuclear facilities and silos. As such, the Air Force in 1952 took the lead in training military working dogs – a role it maintains today.

The Air Force activated its first sentry dog school at Showa Air Station, Japan, in 1952. A second school opened the following year at Wiesbaden, West Germany. Fewer than one-thousand dogs remained in service by 1957. Most were trained in sentry duty. Half were in Europe and about a quarter were in the Far East.

But that would soon change as the United States entered operations in Southeast Asia.

The First Marine Scout Dog Platoon was the first of its kind to arrive in country, landing on March 3 & 4, 1966. It was the first time in more than two decades Marines scout dogs deployed for combat. The Army sent its first two scout dog platoons three months later.

38-39 The American military had no real war dog program at the launch of World War II. By war's end, more than 10,000 dogs received advanced training at five War Dog Reception and Training Centers. German Shepherds and Doberman Pinschers were most often selected for sentry, attack and scout missions.

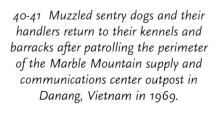

40-41 *Muzzled sentry dogs and their handlers return to their kennels and barracks after patrolling the perimeter of the Marble Mountain supply and communications center outpost in Danang, Vietnam in 1969.*

The ten thousand handlers and more than four thousand dogs to follow soon found service in Vietnam to be far different than in Korea. The night patrols common to Korea were avoided in the booby-trapped jungles, driving dogs to operate in stifling heat. When a three-year-old German Shepherd named Mac fell to heat stroke, he became the first American dog to die in Vietnam. He was not the last. One hundred nine dogs died of heat stroke in 1969 alone.

Heat-related illness and disease such as hookworm and tropical canine pancytopenia proved to be the dogs' greatest enemy. Combat caused fewer than three percent of canine casualties in Vietnam, and accidents accounted for roughly twenty percent.

Dogs also had to contend with malnourishment as food often took so long to arrive that it was rotten upon delivery.

Despite these obstacles, the use and success of canine operations expanded greatly in Vietnam.

Sentry dogs continued to guard fixed installations and scout dogs, typically German Shepherds, were faithful to let troops know when bad guys were nearby. Nearly half of these dogs were assigned to III Corps, which surrounded Saigon.

The war also saw an emphasis on tracker dogs, typically Labrador Retrievers, which were used to follow enemy movements or locate enemy personnel. Thirty dogs provided by the British formed the first fourteen tracker dog teams.

Operation Coronado in August 1966 marked the formal introduction of war dogs for intimidation and interrogation of prisoners. Off-leash patrols, which allow the dog to enter potential ambush sites well ahead of the soldiers, became a dominant tactic in April 1967.

42-43 U.S. Army Specialist Christian Dietz follows his scout dog, "Wolf," out of a flooded rice paddy on July 28, 1968. The team had been looking for enemy troops suspected of moving into Saigon.

Vietnam also saw the rise of detector dogs used to locate mines, tunnels, munitions, booby-traps and narcotics. Much like today's improvised explosive devices, mines and booby traps were the greatest threat for troops in Vietnam. Mine sniffing dogs soon became an invaluable asset – a truth that has exponentially increased during the War on Terror.

So critical was this capability that an Army Concept Team in January 1970 recommended the number of mine dogs be increased by one-hundred fifty percent "to satisfy the greater demand for mine dog support." The report also urged that dog platoons be employed as an integral unit.

The report followed a three-month evaluation of the 60th Infantry Platoon (Mine/Tunnel Detector Dog).

By 1972, Army scout and mine/tunnel dog teams had logged more than eighty-four thousand missions and exposed more than two thousand tunnels and bunkers. They were responsible for more than four thousand enemy being killed and more than one thousand captured. They located untold thousands of weapons including rifles, mines and mortars. The teams relieved the enemy of more than four hundred pounds of documents, one million pounds of rice, three tons of corn and two tons of salt.

But those numbers came at a price. Two-hundred ninety four handlers and three-hundred nine dogs were killed in action.

The Corps' statistics are harder to come by, but one periodical said Marine dog teams from January 1968 to October 1969 detected nearly twelve hundred ambushes and captured more than five hundred enemy soldiers. The dogs also located eighty-six enemy camps, thirty-four enemy hospitals and thirteen radio relay stations, and recovered twenty-three tons of rice, more than thirteen hundred weapons and three-hundred fifty one sets of documents.

Sadly, the Defense Department was ignorant of its own history and would not allow war dogs to be returned home, as it had allowed after World War II. The Pentagon inexplicably declared the dogs to be a threat to society and ordered they be left in Vietnam along with other "equipment" such as helicopters, tanks and trucks.

Most starved to death or were killed and eaten.

The use of military working dogs was largely relegated to base security for the next twenty years, though the British in 1971 started using dogs to detect explosives in Northern Ireland.

Dogs were not used in Operation Urgent Fury, the 1983 U.S.-led invasion of Grenada. The Israeli Special Forces in 1988 drew international ire when it sent bomb-carrying Rottweilers into enemy bunkers in Lebanon. Operation Just Cause, the 1989 invasion of Panama, used a handful of patrol dogs.

The Persian Gulf War, which started massing forces in August 1990, saw a slight resurgence of war dogs. The first dogs to arrive were sent by the First Fighter Wing based at Langley Air Force Base, Va. Roughly one hundred and eighteen U.S. dog teams followed to provide security as well as explosive and narcotic detection. This marked the first combat operation for the Belgian Malinois.

France also deployed more than one thousand German Shepherds to protect its supplies.

Dog teams were in a new location, but soon reunited with two old adversaries. The stifling heat that attacked dogs in World War II and Vietnam and the threat of chemical warfare, which had not been faced since World War I. Handlers carried atropine auto-injectors for their dogs in case such an attack was launched. Other advancements included climate-controlled kennels and specialized glasses to protect the dog's eyes from blowing sand.

The military working dog program saw little change in the decade that followed. But the terrorist attacks of September 11, 2001 changed everything.

Coalition forces fighting in Iraq and Afghanistan were hit by an elusive counterinsurgency unlike anything they had ever seen. Conventional warfare gave way to a hybrid concoction of traditional militants, terrorists and guerillas whose weapon of choice remains the improvised explosive device. A Pentagon that often considered canines to be second-class combatants would soon entrust the teams with the greatest responsibility war dogs have ever known.

With a faithfulness centuries in the making, the war dogs have answered that call.

44-45 U.S. soldier William Reed holds "Sambo," a Labrador Retriever scout dog, in check on Nov. 10, 1967. The team, part of a hawk flight squad from the 1st Air Cavalry Division, was seeking Viet Cong forces near Phong Phu in Vietnam.

46-47 A handler and his scout dog fighting against a strong current during operations west of Saigon on Sept. 13, 1968. The handler, a member of the U.S. 199th Light Infantry Brigade, used cable to work his way across.

THE TRAINING

The elite war dogs of the 21st Century carry the official title of "Military Working Dog" ('MWDs').

These four-legged fighters are trusted by dozens of nations including Italy, Greece, Philippines, Spain, Portugal, Australia, Austria, Turkey and New Zealand.

The role of MWDs varies, but is fairly predictable. For example, Switzerland uses dogs primarily in a search and rescue role, Russia has working dogs at every border post and Mexican MWDs focus on narcotics detection.

Germany has canine platoons consisting of eighteen dog teams in each parachute battalion. Handlers are first fully trained as jump-qualified infantrymen.

Though absent from the wars in Iraq and Afghanistan, Russia has trained more than three thousand military working dogs since 2005. This is compared to only six hundred and ten dogs trained for operations in Afghanistan from 1980 to 1988. Those MWDs located more than seven thousand mines.

Nations that boast the largest working dog populations include the United States, France, Russia and Great Britain – but other countries are close on their heels. The Czech Republic has more than thirteen hundred working dogs and can train as many as six hundred handlers and four hundred and fifty dogs annually. India has several thousand working dogs.

The number of Israel's working dogs is highly classified. They fall into one of three categories: patrol, explosive detection and search and rescue. The Oketz, the Israeli canine Special Forces unit has prevented more than two hundred suicide attacks since 2002.

Similarly, France is tight-lipped about its military working dog programs. But dogs are a key component of all military branches and the French Foreign Legion. The 132nd Battalion of the Canine Army based in Suippes, Marne, has a kennel that houses nearly seven hundred dogs, the largest of its kind in Europe. But it is rarely full – the nation in 2011 had dog teams deployed to Lebanon, Gabon, Guyana, Cote D'Ivoire, Kosovo and Afghanistan.

Even Iraq has come to recognize the working dogs' immeasurable worth.

Many Muslims see dogs as "unclean" animals, but the ability of man's best friend to locate explosives is winning over the population and government. The Iraqi police force looks to put one thousand bomb-sniffing dogs and handlers on the streets by 2015.

Great Britain, on the other hand, has known the worth of war dogs for centuries.

The Defense Animal Centre in Melton Mowbray is home to Britain's Joint Service Dog School, which trains about three hundred dogs each year. Most dogs are donated by the general public and take four to six months to train. The school also offers twenty-two handler courses covering everything from explosive detection to search and protection.

The high demand of these dogs led Great Britain in March 2010 to consolidate five MWD squadrons into the First Military Working Dog Regiment. The regiment's nearly three hundred soldiers and two hundred dogs support world-wide operations from bases in Aldershot (101), North Luffenham (104) and Sennelager, Germany (102, 103 and 105).

49 Two soldiers and war dogs from the 26th Airborne Brigade of the Bundeswehr (German Armed Forces) rappel from a helicopter in Merzig, Southern Germany in June 2006. The teams deployed the following month to the Democratic Republic of Congo for the country's first free elections.

50-51 *Soldiers and war dogs from the Second Foreign Parachute Regiment of the French Foreign Legion train in Calvi, a town on the island of Corsica, just south of mainland France. The unit, part of the 11th Parachute Brigade, serves as the spearhead of the French Rapid Reaction Force.*

51 *War dogs of the Second Foreign Parachute Regiment are trained to be used as combat scouts, sentries and trackers.*

52 A Belarusian soldier trains his war dog in April 2011 at
the Belarusian Defence Ministry near the village of Kolodishchi,
some 30 km (18 miles) east of Minsk. The military trains war
dogs for a variety of tasks such as explosive and drug detection,
and border protection.

53 A blindfolded war dog negotiates a balance beam during
exercises December 2003 at the Belarusian Defence Ministry in
Kolodishchi. The dog training center is considered one of Europe's
best and is able to train more than 100 dogs at a time.

54 A Chinese soldier trains a war dog in January 2006 at a military base in Nanjing, east China's Jiangsu province.

54-55 Another soldier trains his war dog by skipping rope. The Chinese military, the Peoples' Liberation Army, has one of the world's largest war dog programs. More than 10,000 dogs are used for combat patrol, security, explosive detection and search and rescue.

Their American allies have twenty-eight hundred working dogs in the ranks divided into four categories: patrol/explosive detection dogs, patrol/narcotic detection dogs, specialized search dogs and combat trackers. Some military kennels in and around Washington, D.C., also house urban search and rescue dogs.

Patrol dogs are the most common and a far cry from the sentry dogs of the Vietnam era they replaced. Sentry dogs were trained to have a passionate distrust of humans backed by heightened aggression. This worked well when dogs guarded military posts and personnel, but these dogs were not the best partner to have on other missions. Many were unable to even operate with friendly forces because they saw everyone as an enemy and would score a bite whenever possible.

Today's patrol dogs are far more tolerant, for the most part. While some carry a disdain for anyone not their handler, most dogs are well composed and look to the handler to know whether a person is a threat. They can work crowds without becoming hostile or search wide areas without being distracted, but can also be counted on to aggressively attack on command.

Unlike a sentry dog handler, today's handler can end that attack by shouting one word. Sentry dogs often had to be pulled off an attack. The dogs were so aggressive that many handlers had to grasp the throat and carefully block the airway just to get the dog to release.

In addition to patrol work, each dog is certified in narcotics (PNDD) or explosives (PEDD). Narcotic dogs can detect fewer than two grams of drugs such as marijuana, hashish, heroin, methamphetamine, ecstasy and cocaine. Explosive dogs can locate eight different items in concentrations too small to measure.

German Shepherds and Belgian Malinois serve as the primary patrol breeds. This dynamic duo is the pick of the litter because they are intelligent, courageous, dependable, predictable, easily trained, have well-developed senses of hearing and smell, strong endurance, great personalities and can adapt readily to almost any climatic condition.

But natural ability is not enough. The dogs must complete one hundred and twenty days of intense training, half in patrol work and half in detection work, to earn the PEDD or PNDD title.

The specialized search dog has no patrol duties or training. The dog's capacity for sniffing out explosives is instead amplified in a ninety-three day course.

This third MWD category has its origins in North Africa during World War II. The dogs did not do well, finding only about half of planted mines in two tests runs. The adverse conditions were blamed for the poor results.

Mine dogs fared much better in Vietnam and today, SSDs have proven themselves an invaluable asset in locating improvised explosive devices, the number one killer of coalition forces in Iraq and Afghanistan. Since launched in 2005, the SSD program has turned up hundreds of thousands of pounds of weapons, ordnance, explosives and ammunition.

Most SSDs are Labrador Retrievers. They are paired with their handler at the SSD course, graduate together then deploy as a team. The school graduates about fifty dog teams per year that are shared between the Army and Marine Corps.

The Labrador's independent nature enables it to work off-leash, which keeps the handler a safe distance from hidden bombs. The handler maintains control with voice and directional commands.

57 U.S. Marine Lance Cpl. Jose Rivera, a dog handler trained to work with combat trackers, is attacked Oct. 24, 2011, by patrol dogs during a demonstration to students of Condor Elementary School, which is located aboard Marine Corps Air Ground Combat Center Twentynine Palms, California.

The key to success is the dog's sense of smell, called "the olfactory ability." Dogs have two hundred twenty million scent receptors – forty-four times more than humans. To define the strength of that snout, it is often said that when a human smells a baking cake, a dog smells every ingredient contained in that cake. And all of the ingredients on the countertops and in the garbage can.

Bad guys with bombs have spent tons of money trying to defeat the dog's nose, and they continue to come up short. When they try to get away, the Marine Corps' combat tracker dogs are hot on their trail.

The program showed great worth in Vietnam. Tracker dogs were able to detect enemy soldiers with ease because the Asian diet was based on rice, while the American diet is based on wheat. The resulting body odors are quite different to the dog's keen nose.

The forty-day tracker course was restarted in 2010 and graduates about a dozen dog teams each year. Combat trackers can sniff out everything from snipers to missing personnel. The dogs have spoiled ambushes and tracked enemy movements in the combat zone. One of the most useful capabilities is seen after an explosive detector finds a roadside bomb or IED. The combat trackers are called in to pick up a scent and will follow it back to the bomb's delivery boy.

The military looks to specialized European vendors and an in-house breeding program to fill the ranks of these prestigious packs. But not just any dog will do. The military will spend upwards of forty thousand dollars a year to train, treat and house these four-legged fighters and will settle for nothing short of excellence. Officials look for energetic dogs that have a high drive for reward. They must display high levels of courage, concentration and a temperament to learn. Gun shy dogs need not apply.

58-59 A Marine rewards his specialized search dog with a toy. Handlers today use the "Deferred Final Response" which reinforces explosive detection with a reward.

MWD prospects are between one and three years old. They must stand at least twenty-two inches high at the shoulders and have proportional athletic physique. Dogs must also pass in-depth examinations that include radiographs of hips and elbows. This is especially important for German Shepherds, which are prone to a genetic condition called "hip dysplasia," in which the ball will fail to properly fit in the socket as the dog ages. This causes significant pain and possible paralysis, and will cut years off a dog's service.

The Malinois and Shepherds cost about $16,000 each. Tactical explosive detection dogs, which are typically Labrador Retrievers, run $14,000.

Selected dogs are shipped to canine boot camp located at Lackland Air Force Base, near San Antonio, Texas. There, the 341st Training Squadron maintains the world's largest dog training facility. More than five hundred new handlers and three hundred MWDs graduate each year, as well as forty bomb-sniffing dogs that will support combat engineers.

The remarkable success of war dogs at home and abroad can be traced back to Air Force Master Sgt. Richard Reidel. He has trained dogs and handlers throughout the war on terror. As combat operations entered a second decade, the eighteen-year veteran took position as the school's operations superintendent, which put him in charge of the dog training school and the handler, kennel master, combat tracker and specialized search dog courses.

Reidel is quick to salute the one hundred and twenty instructors he has on staff. Like the dogs and handlers they train, only the best candidates are accepted for this special duty assignment. Most have criminal justice degrees or other collegiate-level credentials. Multiple tours to the war zone are not un-

common. The school encourages instructors – who represent all four branches of service – to impart this knowledge and experience in students, as they will likely head to the front lines soon after graduation.

The squadron has ninety training areas covering four hundred acres. It can house one thousand dogs, and typically has about eight hundred and fifty on site.

A $15 million vet hospital stands as a crown jewel. Opened in October 2008, the state-of-the-art facility boasts two surgical operating rooms and two out-patient medical treatment rooms where veterinarians can conduct endoscopy, laparoscopy, arthroscopy, orthopedic and neurosurgery. The latest in advanced imaging is available, such as digital radiography, ultrasound and computed tomography or CAT scans. Once out of the hospital's intensive care unit, dogs are treated to unmatched rehabilitation and physical therapy that utilizes everything from laser therapy to underwater treadmills.

The hospital is staffed by fourteen veterinarians with advanced training in surgery, radiology, internal medicine, critical care, epidemiology and animal behavior. Twenty-five registered veterinary technicians and Army animal care specialists are also on staff.

While compassionate care is a cornerstone for the hospital, obedience is the name of the game on the training fields.

"Deferred Final Response" is the technique used to transform a good dog into a war dog. The old "yank and crank" method had handlers yank the choke chain when the dog did something wrong. The DFR method reinforces positive behavior with a reward. The dog is taught to recognize the target odor and sit when that odor is located. The dog then receives a reward, which becomes its primary motivation for future searches.

61 *Senior Airman Gregory Darby, a military working dog handler from the 8th Security Forces Squadron at Kunsan Air Base, Republic of Korea, shares a quiet moment in 2003 with his dog "Mack." The duo had completed the obstacle course at an Operation Enduring Freedom location.*

As such, a dog is not looking for narcotics or explosives – the dog is looking for a reward. The narcotics or explosives are just the means to an end.

The reward usually is a combination of verbal praise, petting and a treat or toy. The dogs, now driven by reward, are ignored when they ignore a command or fail to properly carry it out. Further correction is rarely required. If necessary, handlers will give a jerk on the leash with a firm "No!" They are never allowed to inflict pain on a dog.

Once this foundation is laid, dogs are ready for advance training in controlled aggression. Dogs are taught to attack – and withdraw – when ordered, and they learn to protect their handler. This is an easy lesson for most dogs, and especially patrol dogs. The handler is parent, provider and best friend to the dog, and they will protect that person at all cost. This defense mechanism is so intense that handlers use code words or cues to let the canine know whether the situation is okay. If not conveyed when a person approaches the handler, the dog will quickly stand up and emit a threatening growl through forty-two exposed teeth. If the cue still does not come, the person will quickly learn the dog's bite is worse than his bark.

62 Petty Officer 2nd Class Gina Pronzati, with Task Force Military Police, rewards her military working dog, "Dicky," for completing his training mission in November 2007 in Camp Fallujah, Iraq.

63 A chief Master-at-Arms, attached to the Naval Security Force K-9 Unit in Bahrain trains with his Belgian Malinois in May 2007. The detection training is held at least three times per month so war dogs stay adept at detecting explosive odors.

Before hitting the streets, dogs are taught two methods of controlled aggression. The Six Phases method has half a dozen key components:

The False Run When commanded to "Stay!" the dog must remain in the heel, sit or down position, off–leash, and not attack when a person approaches the team.

False Run into a Bite Picking up from the previous scenario, the dog must attack on the command of "Get Him!" The dog is taught to bite and hold for fifteen seconds and release on the command "Out!" The handler can give the command twice. If the dog does not release, he fails. The dog must also return to its handler when commanded to "Heel!"

Search and Attack The off–leash dog remains in the heel, down, or sit position while the handler searches a suspect. The dog must attack without command if the suspect tries to escape or attacks the handler. The handler will then move to position the suspect between himself and the dog. The handler will face the dog and give the command to "Heel!" To return to his master's side, the dog has to walk past the bad guy without biting him again.

Search and Call By This is identical to the previous scenario, except the suspect will not resist and the dog must not attack.

Stand-off A dog will be given one command to "Get Him!" The handler yells "Out!" as the dog draws

64 Master-at-Arms 2nd Class David Nerling gives the hand command "down" to his military working dog "Valerie" during basic obedience training in August 2006 at Lackland Air Force Base, Texas. Nerling is a military working dog trainer with the 341st Training Squadron and works jointly with Air Force, Army and Marine dog trainers.

near the suspect. The dog must immediately cease his pursuit without biting and return on the command of "Heel!"

Escort The team must escort a suspect for at least twenty yards without attacking.

"Out and Guard" is the second method of controlled aggression. It has eight key components. The first five are similar to the actions taught in "Six Phases," but this method also adds:

Building search The dog must find a suspect inside any structure, and show the handler where the decoy is located.

Gunfire The dog must show it is not adversely affected by gunfire, either when the handler or another person is firing. In addition, the dog must not attack when it hears gunfire.

Scouting or patrolling The dog must show it is able to find people by scent, sight or sound. Search subjects hide between one hundred and two hundred yards upwind.

If the dog can meet these stands – and more than ninety percent will, thanks to the stringent recruitment standards – the canine will earn the right to be called a "Military Working Dog." He will be entrusted with the protection of military bases, personnel and their families. He will protect lawmakers, presidents and foreign dignitaries. He will find terrorists and IEDs on the front lines of combat.

65 *Both verbal and nonverbal commands are used to train Military Working Dogs at the 341st Training Squadron at Lackland Air Force Base, Texas. More than 1,300 dogs from each service branch are trained there annually for patrol and bomb/drug detection.*

And his training will never stop. Each dog's capabilities will remain razor sharp, and he will always be pushed to new levels. He has the kennel master to thank for that.

No matter how long a dog has served, how loud he barks or how hard he bites, the kennel master will always be the Alpha Dog in a Military Working Dog unit.

The kennel master has oversight of all dogs and handlers at his base or post. He is responsible for the dogs' feeding, veterinary care, training and deployments. He ensures all dog teams are fully certified and at the top of their game. He manages the unit's budget and facilities. He also advises the command on how MWD teams are best used in the respective environment.

The kennel master is no pup. He is at least an E-6 in rank (a Marine or Army staff sergeant, an Air Force technical sergeant or a Navy petty officer first class). He must have at least four successful years as a handler, though most have far more. He must also graduate the seventeen-day Kennel Master Course taught at Lackland Air Force Base.

Perhaps the most important task for the kennel master is to ensure his handlers are the very best they can be, and that they bring out the very best in each dog. This skill is honed daily.

The first step is to allow the dog and handler to bond. This is the foundation upon which every team is built – and it sometimes requires some innovative thinking.

Sgt. 1st Class William Webster in 2005 got orders for duty in Afghanistan. He was assigned an intimidating PEDD named "Lucky." The first time Webster greeted "Lucky", the dog responded with a deep scowl that revealed all his teeth. No growl, no bark, just forty-two teeth and a bad attitude. Worse yet, the dog's front four teeth were titanium – the result of him using a steel bowl as a chew toy.

Webster arrived at the kennel the next day to begin the bonding process. So notorious was "Lucky"'s aggression that other handlers fixed the closed caption cameras on his run so they could watch the show. But this was not Webster's first rodeo. He coated his hand with crushed pepperoni treats and entered with confidence. He grabbed "Lucky"'s choke chain then put the pepperoni-covered hand in the dog's face. "Lucky" started licking, Webster started petting and the bond was made.

A new team like Webster and "Lucky" will spend about two weeks getting to know each other. The handler will groom, feed and play with the dog, and the canine will come to trust his handler for everything he needs.

The bond that results is expressed differently by each team. Some dogs jump up and give their handlers a kiss upon seeing them. Some nudge against the handler's legs. Others simply sit and wag their tail, but refuse to even give a hug until they have been fed. Just like their handlers, each dog has a distinct personality.

Handlers value that devotion and protection, and show their appreciation at the start of every work day. The deep trust and friendship shared is evident, but there is greater purpose behind this playful period. The handler uses this one-on-one time to carefully check the dog's health, with a special focus on the eyes, nose, ears, mouth, skin, fur, genitals and anal glands.

67 "Gunner" is comforted by his handler, U.S. Marine Cpl. Chad McCoy, in February 2010 at Camp Leatherneck in the Helmand Province of Afghanistan. McCoy and other handlers diagnosed "Gunner" with the canine version of PTSD after the explosive detector became skittish and started to run from the sound of explosions.

The dog is then treated to a balanced breakfast of Hill's Science Diet Active Maintenance Formula. The dry food includes corn meal, chicken by-products, animal fat, vegetable oil, dried egg, flaxseed and a vitamin variety. These canine athletes need this high-nutrition diet to meet the rigorous requirements placed on them. Vets use each dog's weight, activity and climate to determine the proper amount of food, which usually runs between one to four cups.

Doggie bags are not allowed. Leftovers are quickly taken up, but each dog will get to eat later in the day. This cycle will limit the amount of gas the dogs produce, which could cause a potentially fatal case of bloating. This happens when air and gases become trapped in the stomach of larger dogs and cut off circulation to the stomach and spleen.

Every MWD also undergoes a gastropexy, or stapling of the stomach to the side of the rib cage, to further reduce the risk.

The dog will have about two hours to eat. Handlers use this time to groom the dog and administer veterinarian-prescribed medication, which could be capsule, topical or liquid. Once breakfast has settled the dogs get to stretch their legs.

Handlers first loosen the dog's joints at the obstacle course. The canines show their strength and agility as they jump hurdles, run stairs, climb through windows and crawl through tunnels with ease. Handlers closely monitor every movement to identify any physical problems that may have risen.

Next come centerline drills, which closely resemble a game of fetch. The drills exercise verbal obedience commands that are a hallmark of MWD opera-

tions. Shouts of *"Down! Heel! Sit! and Out!"* echo across the kennel as each dog is put through the paces. One handler likened it to warming up a car on a cold winter morning. The dog must be "warmed up and running in the right frame of mind" to ensure it will closely listen and quickly respond to given commands.

68 U.S. Air Force Staff Sgt. Jason Albrecht runs "Markey" through an obstacle course on July 13, 2011, at Shaw Air Force Base, S.C. Albrecht is a senior military working dog handler assigned to the 20th Security Forces Squadron.

68-69 U.S. Air Force Staff Sgt. Derek Donahey monitors his military working dog, "Oran," as he jumps through a mock window at the Nellis Air Force Base, Nev., obstacle course. Donahey and Oran are security forces members with the 99th Security Forces Squadron.

70 *A British soldier from the Theater Military Working Dog Unit train a German Shepherd war dog on September 29, 2004, at the British base in Shaibah near Basrah in Southern Iraq. The support unit had German Shepherd attack dogs and Labrador or English Springier Spaniels trained to find explosives.*

71 *Master-at-Arms 2nd Class Jeremy Aldrich, attached to the Naval Security Force K-9 Unit in Bahrain, and his Military Working Dog "Tyson," a four-year-old blue Belgian Malinois, take a break on May 7, 2007, at the base obstacle course. Aldrich worked with "Tyson" for 18 months in support of the mission to provide security to the base and the Mina Salman pier.*

72-73 A Marine starts the mission by loosening his German Shepherd's joints at the obstacle course. Dogs will tackle tunnels, jump hurdles, run stairs and climb through windows. This also helps the handler identify any physical problems the canine may have.

73 U.S. Air Force Staff Sgt. Chris Reynolds runs his German Shepherd, "Baiky," through a training obstacle course Aug. 7, 2009 at Bagram Airfield, Afghanistan. Reynolds, an eight-year veteran, is a dog handler with the 455th Expeditionary Security Forces Squadron.

Once in the right frame of mind, the team turns to the aggression training for which canines are best known. A popular training technique has the handler approach and search a suspect. The dog will keep an intimidating eye on the shady character throughout, and launches into action like a rocket the moment the bad guy fights or flees. Another popular scenario sends the dog into a building or wood line to find a hiding suspect. The search usually ends before the perpetrator knows what hit him.

And this is no game for the dog. He trains as he fights, at one-hundred percent. Having a canine athlete attack you at full speed is brutal in its own right. The force of the impact knocks most grown men off their feet. But it is the bite that leaves the lasting scars. Even with a thick protective pad, seven hundred pounds of pressure per square inch feels like a pair of giant vice grips clamped on and twisting your arm.

Such aggression training is so physically demanding that teams limit it to three times a week to ensure muscles have time to recuperate – for the dog and the handler who played the role of the bad guy.

74 and 74-75 Lance Cpl. Drew Nyman, a working dog handler with the Combat Center's Provost Marshal's Office and a native of Emporia, Kan., works on take-down techniques with Robby, a Military Working Dog with PMO July 27, 2009. A war dog bite exerts between 400 and 700 pounds of pressure per square inch.

76 77 "Rocky," a Military Working Dog, grabs onto a biting wrap worn by U.S. Navy Master-at-Arms 2nd Class Adam Leeds during an Oct. 10, 2006 canine demonstration on Naval Support Activity Bahrain. The demonstration was to show the armed forces community the capabilities of Naval police dogs.

Once the canine athlete has taken that bite out of crime, the soldier athlete gets ready for his own physical training. Handlers have to meet the same strenuous physical requirements as every other service member, so the handler and dog partner up to run a few miles of cross-country trails or swim laps at the base pool. The key is to do it in the morning so the dog does not overheat.

78 An Air Force sergeant prepares to let his Military Working Dog search off-leash. This technique allows dogs to enter potential ambush sites well ahead of soldiers aned keeps handlers at a safe distance from hidden bombs.

79 top and bottom U.S. Air Force Staff Sgt. Erick Martinez uses an over-the-shoulder carry with "Argo II," during an exercise at Hill Air Force Base, Utah. In the same way Military Working Dogs protect soldiers from the enemy and explosives, handlers must be able to carry their partner when the dog becomes exhausted or wounded.

As most people are just getting settled in at work, the dog team is getting ready to tackle the next task: Detection training.

Each team must conduct four hours of detection training every week, except SSDs, which are required to log six hours. The dogs are not graded on a curve — only excellence is accepted. Explosive detectors must find ninety-five percent of explosives while narcotic dogs must find nine out of ten items. Neither dog can have more than a ten-percent false response rate.

The kennel master assigns a separate trainer to set up these exercises. The scenarios are limited only by his imagination. Items may be hidden in backpacks or barracks, in a home or on the highway. The handler has no idea where the drugs or explosives are planted in the search area. Otherwise, he may have a tendency to focus on those areas — or away from those areas in an effort to trick the dog. Having a separate trainer hide the items lets the handler and dog better "read" each other to know how each will act in a real environment.

Trainers use this time to make the handler better. They carefully watch the handler's pace, body language, mannerisms and commands. Young handlers, for example, have a tendency to confuse the dog with behavior that suggests a reward is coming when it is not.

Handlers, in turn, use detection training to "learn" their dogs. The MWD is not a robot. It is very smart and will sometimes try to get a reward by mimicking positive behaviors. A good handler will not be fooled, and will keep the dog on task.

Handlers also use this time to overcome the dog's fears and bad habits and make no mistake, all dogs have something to overcome. Some get "lazy" on searches and will not go low or high. Some get spooked by mirrors because they think it is another dog. Others are scared by loud noises generated by things such as airplanes and helicopters.

"Domil," a German Shepherd at Fort Benning,

Georgia, was afraid of televisions. The narcotics detector is a combat veteran that has proven his worth time and again, but he would not go near a TV.

His handler, Army Specialist Tabra Carn, has no idea why her dog reacted this way, but she used her daily detection time to help him get over his fear. She worked "Domil" with a TV in the distance, and gradually brought him closer. When he hesitated,

Carn would play with "Domil" and affirm him with an enthusiastic "*Good boy!*" His fear subsided in a matter of weeks.

This detection training wraps up in the early afternoon. The dog relaxes about an hour before eating dinner while the handler updates a detailed account of the day's activities. Every little detail is carefully documented throughout a dog's life.

80-81 The dog's sense of smell, called "the olfactory ability," can alert troops to enemy personnel and explosives that would otherwise go unnoticed. Dogs have two hundred twenty million scent receptors — forty-four times more than humans.

When the log book closes, the training day has come to an end but it is not time to turn off the lights and head home - not by a long shot.

PEDDs and PNDDs must conduct at least four hours of patrol every week and 96 hours of utilization each month. This could be in law enforcement or other special missions. For example, MWDs provide routine assistance to nearby communities that do not have dog programs of their own. They also support Secret Service missions when senior military or government officials are in the area. In these missions, it is quickly evident that MWDs are in a class of their own. Intense training and combat operations have built dogs that outlast and outperform Secret Service dogs, and the dark-suited men in charge of security know it. It is not uncommon for a detail agent to ask an MWD team to sweep an area that a Secret Service dog has already hit or to cover an area the Secret Service dog is unable to cover due to exhaustion.

MWD teams must also pass annual certification amid this grueling pace. This certification is also required if a handler gets a new dog, the team has not conducted sustainment training for thirty-five consecutive days or the team fails to reach detection rates for two consecutive months.

Teams travel to a different base to be certified. There, a regional trainer will plant explosives or narcotics in at least five locations. And some locations will have nothing, just to keep the team on its toes. Teams also are tested in confrontational management and crowd control. The goal is to use the least amount of force possible while presenting a physiological deterrence.

Such training is necessary and is respected among law enforcement and military leaders alike, but it leaves the dogs in a hairy predicament when it comes time to retire.

Working dogs typically serve ten to twelve years, though statistics show that dogs frequently deployed in the grueling war zone are forced to retire about eighteen months earlier.

The Robby Law, enacted in 2000, allows these dogs to be adopted. Dogs must pass an in-depth screening process that includes a medical examination and assessment of the dog's temperament before adoption is approved. Some have ailments in their old age that disqualify them from adoption. Others cannot seem to shed their aggressive nature.

About fifteen percent of MWDs come up for adoption annually. Federal law gives priority to law enforcement agencies. Nine out of ten dogs that do not meet age or fitness standards for continued service with civilian law enforcement will be adopted by their handlers. The rest will be adopted by members of the general public who are put on a twelve-month waiting list.

More recently, families of fallen soldiers have been allowed to adopt the dog with which their loved one served.

83 A U.S. Special Forces soldier pets a military working dog on the flight line during exercise Emerald Warrior at Hurlburt Field, Fla., March 7, 2011. Emerald Warrior is an annual two-week joint/combined tactical exercise sponsored by U.S. Special Operations Command designed to leverage lessons learned from operations Iraqi and Enduring Freedom to provide trained and ready forces to combatant commanders.

CHAPTER 2

THE MISSIONS IN AFGHANISTAN AND IRAQ

Dog teams were little more than gate jockeys in the years leading up to the War on Terror. Patrol Explosive Detection Dogs had occasional deployments to places like Bosnia and Kosovo and a handful of narcotic dogs helped on the Texas/Mexico border.

All of that changed on September 11, 2001.

Special Forces Operational Detachment Alpha 555, the "Triple Nickel," was the first group of American servicemen to land in Afghanistan. The A-team hit the Panjshir Valley on October 19 with orders to liberate Bagram Air Base and Kabul. Pentagon planners estimated it would take the team six months. It took only twenty-five days.

The first dog teams to arrive in country were close on the A-team's heels. U.S. Air Force Staff Sgt. Timothy Miller and "Marco" are credited as being the first team in theater. They deployed in September 2001 to an Uzbekistan airbase. As the A-team pressed south from Bagram toward the capital city, Miller and "Marco" joined three hundred 10th Mountain Division soldiers as they cleared and protected the embattled Bagram airbase. They later helped clear the U.S. Embassy in Kabul of explosives.

The dog team was a popular pair, especially in Bagram. Countless mines left from the war with Russia littered the landscape. Even the berms meant to protect friendly forces were filled with explosive surprises. The only safe place to walk was on concrete, and soldiers stepped softly even there.

"Marco"'s missions were a sign of things to come. The number of U.S. Military Working Dogs increased from thirteen hundred to twenty-eight hundred in the decade that followed. Iraq and Afghanistan have seen as many as twelve hundred dog teams in theater at one time.

Kennels support five regional commands in Afghanistan: North, South, Southwest, East and West. Kennels in Iraq support each of the six military sectors, called "Multi-National Divisions:" North, North Central, Baghdad, West, Central South and Southeast.

Dog teams from all the major coalition nations have made repeated deployments in support of these operations. And they have been joined by some smaller, but equally capable dog teams from nations such as The Royal Netherlands, Estonia, Norway, Hungary, Slovenia and Croatia.

Kennel masters typically assigned dogs to divisions within the area of responsibility, though assignments to brigades or regiments were not uncommon.

Unlike Vietnam, where dogs were deployed for the duration, dog and handler are now certified together before heading into theater. They come home together as well. However, dogs often come home for six months of certification with a new handler before deploying again. As a result, most dogs have more deployments under their collar than soldiers have under their belts.

That is not to say the handlers have it easy. They deploy more often and longer than most soldiers. In 2011, the U.S. Army reduced deployments to nine months. But dog teams — in high demand and low numbers — continued to deploy for at least one year at a time.

85 U.S. Marine Cpl. Matthew Flaherty, a Military Working Dog handler with Headquarters and Service Company, 1st Battalion, 25th Marine Regiment, posts security with "Chica," an IED detection dog, during a shura held at a bazaar located outside of Camp Leatherneck, Helmand province on Sept. 29, 2011. The meeting was held to determine how to move squatters located outside of the base to a more secure location farther north.

86-87 *A war dog accompanies a Royal Engineers' patrol from their base in Nahr-e Saraj village to search for Improvised Explosive Devices (IEDs) in the area of Helmand province on June 21, 2010. The British death toll in the Afghan conflict rose to three hundred later that day.*

Those deployments are often a lonely job. Handlers are dropped off on a strange airfield with six hundred pounds of gear and a war dog with a serious case of jet lag. It does not get any easier when the team gets to its unit. Soldiers there have built a strong camaraderie in the yearlong preparatory training that preceded the combat tour. While soldiers are friendly, and even appreciative, a dog team attached to a unit is like a stranger invited to a family reunion simply because he has a utensil the family needs.

"Attached" is the key word. The team may be "attached" to a unit, but that does not mean they are a "part" of the unit. Not yet. The newly attached dog team will not enjoy the support structure other soldiers come to expect. The unit will provide basics such as chow and a cot. But a handler must learn to "wheel and deal" to get things such as a climate-controlled area for the dog or uniforms replaced.

88 A U.S. Marine dog handler from Fox Company, 2nd Battalion, 3rd Marines rests on his dog "Patrick" as his platoon settles into a makeshift patrol base on October 7, 2009.

88-89 Royal Army Veterinary Corp Lance Cpl. Marianne Hay, and her explosive detection dog "Leanna" rest at the Kandahar Air Field shortly before strike operation Southern Beast on August 3, 2008.

90-91 *U.S. Army Sgt. Adam Rainville holds his war dog as soldiers from the 4th Infantry Division watch the Alabama vs Arkansas football game from their military outpost in southern Baghdad on Sept. 20, 2008. The rest was disrupted moments later when the platoon was called to perform a mission.*

91 *U.S. Marines attached to 1st Battalion, 6th Regiment relax as bomb sniffer "Buttom" drinks water in Huskers camp on the outskirts of Marjah in central Helmand, Afghanistan, on Jan. 25, 2010.*

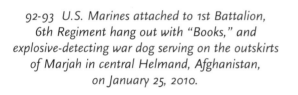
92-93 *U.S. Marines attached to 1st Battalion, 6th Regiment hang out with "Books," and explosive-detecting war dog serving on the outskirts of Marjah in central Helmand, Afghanistan, on January 25, 2010.*

94-95 and 95 A U.S. soldier deployed to the combat zone is able to give his war dog a rare treat: a shower. Water is often rationed in the war zone, and showers are rare. A few moments under cold water was nothing like the grooming experience one might have at the local pet store, but it was a refreshing moment for the dog.

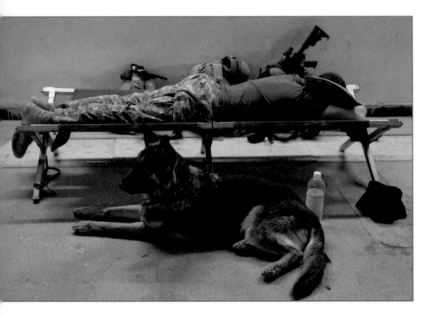

96 A U.S. soldier from the Second Stryker Cavalry Regiment sleeps next to his war dog in Iraq's Diyala province on August 6, 2008. Dogs remain close to their handlers at all times. This was especially critical in the early days of the Afghanistan war, when landmines were everywhere and one wrong step by a curious canine could prove disastrous.

96-97 U.S. Army Sergeant Nathan Arriaga catches some sleep with "Zzarr," a 6-year old Dutch Shepherd on July 24, 2011 at the Forward Operating Base Walton. The team stepped out on patrol in Afghanistan's Arghandab district soon after. Both "Zzarr," an explosive detection dog, and his handler did their first combat duty in Iraq in 2009.

98-99 and 99 U.S. soldiers and one war dog from 2nd Platoon, Charlie Company, 1-75 Cavalry, 2nd Brigade, 101st Airborne Division rest following a patrol in the Siah Choi area of Zari district of Kandahar province, south of Afghanistan on October 23, 2010. The district is the birthplace of the Taliban movement and 2010 was the deadliest year for coalition forces in the region. But operations such as the one pictured here broke that control.

100-101 U.S. Army Sgt. Marcus Mayward is licked by a war dog trained to sniff for explosives inside a military vehicle during security operations in Diyala province Aug. 7, 2008. Al Qaeda had regrouped in Diyala after being routed by U.S. and Iraqi forces in Baghdad and Western Iraq. This team was part of a major security operation to crush insurgents.

101 Handlers and war dogs build a strong camaraderie in the yearlong preparatory training that precedes a combat tour. Once in theater, the dogs become great friends, listeners and confidants. A wagging tail and the lick of your face always brightens even the toughest days.

102 *Soldiers often operate in remote locations, and war dogs are no exception. More than 1,000 were serving at one time in Iraq and Afghanistan in 2011, covering every mission imaginable.*

Sometimes he will have to escalate his efforts when the dog's life is on the line.

Such was the case for Sgt. 1st Class Chad Jones. His dog, "Bo," took shrapnel when two rocket-propelled grenades hit the kennel at Abu Ghraib, Iraq, in May 2005. It was part of a complex attack designed to overrun the combat outpost.

Jones ran through a hail of explosions and small arms fire to get back to the kennel. Another rocket-propelled grenade hit just after Jones entered. The thunderous blast spewed such force that that a fellow handler was convinced Jones lay dead in the fire and smoke that once had been a makeshift kennel.

Jones was alive, but his Belgian Malinois was gone. "Bo" was a gunfire-induced dog, which means the sound of gunfire caused him to react aggressively. A veteran of hundreds of missions, the dog had fought hard to break through a plywood

barrier. He succeeded, but the effort caused significant injuries to his paws.

"Bo" was located a short time later, unable to walk any further. An Army veterinarian in central Baghdad ordered "Bo" taken to the closest triage facility possible. Once stabilized, the one-hundred pound dog was taken by helicopter to the Green Zone cache. The vet, joined by another vet and two veterinary technicians, met the team there. Jones felt a comfortable hope arise, but that hope was soon challenged.

The hospital's officer in charge intercepted "Bo" and entourage at the emergency room. He dutifully told them the dog was not allowed in the hospital because he would "contaminate the facility."

Jones had braved gunfire and explosions to save his dog, and he was not about to let him die now. The handler, covered in the filth of combat and the blood of his dog, gave the major a personal introduction to the passionate bond shared between dog and handler. Jones' words were pointed, though not necessarily professional or polite. But there was no time for courtesy. His fellow soldier was hanging in the balance.

One of the vets jumped in as the discussion intensified, not so much to save Jones but to save "Bo." The captain explained that "Bo" would not contaminate anything. Very few infectious or zoonotic diseases can be transmitted from dogs to humans, and many are mitigated through vaccinations and antibiotic regimens given to deployed working dogs.

The major relented and "Bo" went into surgery. He remained in the Green Zone at a small boarding facility for wounded and recovering dogs for about a month. Once cleared, "Bo" and Jones took the first convoy back to Abu Ghraib where they resumed their duties and fulfilled their mission.

While unfortunate, it is worth noting that Jones' experience is the exception, not the rule. Most medical professionals respond well to the urgency conveyed by a distraught handler and will do whatever they can to help a four-legged soldier.

In one case, a working dog and several service members were seriously injured when an improvised explosive device caused a building to collapse upon them. An evacuation helicopter took all the injured to the Air Force theater hospital in Balad, where dog and human were treated side-by-side.

And sometimes, having the dog at one's side becomes a handler's dying wish.

Lance Cpl. William Crouse and his dog, "Cane," were hit by a roadside bomb days before Christmas in 2010. The 22-year-old Marine's dying plea was that the helicopter crew save his wounded dog. "Cane" did not survive. He was the fifth Marine dog to die from roadside bomb blasts in Afghanistan.

Crouse's example is why handlers train medics and corpsman to treat the dog when they attach to a unit. Still, the handler has no guarantee that medical help will be available in times of need. That is why handlers are taught to treat everything from fractures and heat injuries to burns and snakebite. They are even qualified to provide the dog artificial respiration.

Army Sgt. Sean Wess is glad he got such advanced training. Things were bad enough when a June 2011 patrol suddenly erupted into a "run and gun" fight. Then, without warning, his dog bloated. "Max" was an older Dutch Shepherd whose stomach had not been stapled. Air and gases had become trapped in his stomach and he was fading fast. "Max" would die if his handler did not act.

Wess, who was under fire, decompressed "Max"'s stomach by inserting a tube into his chest cavity. The procedure acts much like a tracheotomy, but in reverse. It was enough to get "Max" stabilized. A "dust off," or medical evacuation by air was called in, and "Max" survived to fight another day.

Getting a wounded dog like "Max" flown out is not too difficult. Getting dog food flown in can prove maddening. It is hard to find room on aircraft packed with combat essentials. Of course, having dog food delivered is not even an option when you are on a forty-day operation in the middle of nowhere.

Sgt. 1st Class William Webster learned to improvise in 2005 when he and his PEDD, "Lucky," conducted such missions with the 82nd Airborne Division in Afghanistan. Webster would take as much food as he could, and an extra twenty dollars for emergencies. He could get five chickens for two dollars from local vendors, and a twenty-pound bag of rice for ten dollars. "Lucky" would eat a cup of rice and as much chicken as Webster would give him. The rest would be saved in the vehicles' coolers.

Finding food can indeed be tough, but finding water can be a battle.

Water rationing is not uncommon in Afghanistan and Iraq. Supplies often run low, especially when water trucks fall prey to an enemy ambush. In such circumstances, soldiers will receive one, maybe two water bottles a day. That is for consumption, bathing, shaving ... everything they need. When the heat index reaches one hundred and twenty degrees in July and August, and a soldier loses a quart of water an hour from sweating, water is an extra precious commodity some supply sergeants are not eager to share with dogs.

Even when water is scarce, explosives are plentiful. Yet finding explosives can be as hard as finding water if the command does not understand the dog's purpose and worth.

Most leaders are eager to get maximum use of the team. Others are not so inclined. They see the team as a labor-intensive burden they have to feed and house. And some young officers do not care to be instructed by an enlisted handler on the proper and necessary employment of dog teams.

Jones recounted a time in Iraq when the captain to whom he was assigned ordered his infantry soldiers to search vehicles for explosives. The Fort Belvoir kennel master explained how his dog could do the job ten times better and ten times faster. The captain said "thanks, but if I need you to bite someone I'll call for you." Jones and his dog went back and sat in the Mine Resistant Ambush Protected vehicle, or MRAP, while the soldiers continued their search.

Such challenges are unfortunate, but they also build a stronger bond between dog and handler. War dogs are great friends, listeners and confidants. And after a bad day, a wagging tail and the lick of your face has a way of making things a little better. And inevitably, there comes "the moment." It is the moment the team is able to show its stuff. The moment in which every commander becomes a believer and the unit welcomes the team into the family. For Army Sgt. Chris Bond, the moment came after he volunteered for a walking patrol with the 4th Infantry Division.

104 A U.S. Army handler shares water with his dog in Muqdadiyah, Iraq. It is difficult to get basic supplies when deployed.

105 A U.S. Army dog handler gives his Military Working Dog water during operations, June 18, 2007, in Saqlawiyah, Iraq.

106-107 U.S. Army Sgt. Joshua Smith provides water to his Military Working Dog, "Blacky."

108-109 A war dog crosses a wadi alongside his handler during a combat patrol.

110-111 *U.S. Air Force Sgt. Matthew Templet, of the 627th Security Forces Squadron at Joint Base Lewis-McChord, Wash., gives encouragement to "Basco" on Dec. 28, 2010. The Patrol Explosive Detector Dog was tasked with checking a dark tunnel for explosives in an abandoned house in the Zari district of Kandahar province.*

It was the winter of 2008 and the unit was securing the area outside the embattled Joint Security Station Sadr City, located in a Baghdad suburb east of the Tigris River.

Bond, originally placed in the middle of the formation, was able to convince the well-meaning platoon sergeant to move him to "point" at the front of the patrol. Things did not go well at first. Bond's German Shepherd, "Dak," suddenly came down with diarrhea and headed off route every few minutes to take care of business. The repeated stops frustrated and embarrassed the handler. But "Dak"'s drive was different the fifth time he veered off course. He went straight for a trash pile and alerted. A Styrofoam box with protruding wires was found buried in the garbage. It was an "EFP" — an explosively formed penetrator designed to pierce armor.

111 U.S. Air Force Sgt. Matthew Templet and "Basco" search an abandoned house for explosives in Haji Ghaffar village during a clearance patrol in Zari district of Kandahar province on Dec. 27, 2010. Residents left the village when it became a battlefield against Taliban.

112-113 "Dazz" prepares to sniff out a suspected IED on a training exercise with his handler Cpl. Tony Bryson from the Royal Vetrinary Corps. The exercise was held at the EOD training ground in Camp Bastion, Helmand, Afghanistan.

"Somebody went home and sat with his family at Christmas because of that," Bond said.

Indeed, there comes "the moment" when everyone becomes a believer. But some come to that understanding the hard way.

Just ask Webster. He and "Lucky" were tasked to search a mountain cave on the Pakistan border soon after they were assigned to 2nd Battalion, 504th Parachute Infantry Regiment, 82nd Airborne Division. They progressed so deep that Webster and "Lucky" were barely able to crawl through the narrow passage. Webster decided to pull back and head out. "Lucky" showed interest as they navigated through the pitch darkness. Webster placed his hand on "Lucky"'s head and felt his ears were pointed forward. Somehow, someone had got behind them.

Webster shouted a warning then released "Lucky"'s leash with an emphatic *Get him!* The German Shepherd quickly obliged. Moments later Webster and two soldiers assigned as his security heard clothes ripping as someone shouted in clear and profanity-laced English to call off the dog.

"*Out! Heel!*" Webster yelled into the darkness. The handler decided the area was secure and called for "white light" to assess the situation. He saw the company commander before him. The captain had failed to let the team know he was coming, and was a bit war-torn as a result. "Lucky" continued to stare at the commander with intent, ready to pounce again if the officer decided to move.

"Sorry, sir," Webster said.

In that moment, the captain made a mistake he would not repeat, and met a weapon he would often use.

And it is the anticipation of such moments that make teams unwilling to remain in the rear with the gear. This attitude is evident by the price dog teams pay.

Improvised Explosive Devices are responsible for more than half of coalition troops killed.

114-115 *U.S. Air Force dog handler Staff Sgt. Justin Schwartz climbs a mountainside behind his bomb-sniffing dog "Bleck" October 14, 2009 in Paktika Province, Afghanistan.*

Seven hundred and eighty-nine troops were killed by IEDs and another eight thousand seven hundred and seventeen were wounded in Afghanistan through September 2011. In the same period in Iraq, two thousand two hundred and twenty five were killed and twenty-one thousand seven hundred and twenty-seven were wounded.

June and July 2011 saw the highest number of IED events in ten years of combat in Afghanistan, followed by a slight decrease in August. When compared to the same three-month period in 2010, IED events increased twenty six percent and averaged nearly seventeen hundred per month. The number of IED attacks against dismounted troops also increased ninety-two percent in the same period.

The Joint Improvised Explosive Device Defeat Organization, or JIEDDO, spent $16.6 billion from 2006 to September 2010 to defeat the IED. It tested every technology imaginable, but insurgents work hard to stay one step ahead. As a result, the ability to find IEDs and jam detonation commands has remained at about fifty percent throughout the War on Terror.

But war dogs stand as one weapon the bad guys cannot beat. When dogs are in the operation, the IED detection rate jumps to as high as eighty percent.

In the words of retired Gen. David Petraeus, "The capability that military working dogs bring to the fight cannot be replicated by man or machine. By all measures of performance, their yield outperforms any asset we have in our inventory. Our Army would be remiss if we failed to invest more in this incredibly valuable resource."

Petraeus served from 2008 to 2010 as commander of United States Central Command, which oversees military efforts in twenty countries including Iraq, Iran, Afghanistan, Pakistan and Egypt. He retired in 2011 to head the Central Intelligence Agency.

Today, three out of four IEDs in Afghanistan use fertilizer-based homemade explosives, or HMEs, as the main charge. In response, JIEDDO and military kennels send war dogs to places such as the CIA's special mission compound, where they learn to detect very minute portions of preferred explosives such as sugar potassium, ammonium nitrate, potassium chlorate and urea nitrate. But there is an element far more dangerous than any ingredient the enemy may use. It is the complacency that comes when these repeated mission become routine for IED hunters.

"The first time you have an alert, you know you're in the real deal," said Army Sgt. John Hawkings, who served Afghanistan's Kandahar Province with his PEDD Whiskey in 2010 and 2011.

"Time goes into slow motion. You can feel your heart beat through your rib cage. You can feel every trickle of sweat rolling down your forehead and arms and back."

His team conducted multiple missions daily in places like the Argonaut Valley, Maiwand and Zhari. Hawkings said it does not take long before finding IEDs becomes routine, and if not careful, "routine results in death."

The search for IEDs is not the only dangerous mission to which war dogs are assigned. Dog teams help clear buildings and vehicles, they provide security in the world's most dangerous places and they sweep government buildings for the host nation. The teams are so effective that the mere presence of dogs can have a remarkable effect – even if the dogs are decoys.

Maj. Gen. Robert Brown in 2010 became the commander of the Army's Maneuver Center of Excellence at Fort Benning, Georgia. But in 2007 he commanded forces in and around Mosul, Iraq.

Countless roads and paths gave the enemy easy access to the city of two and a half million people. Brown shut the door and established twelve hard entrances with manned checkpoints. He knew the bad guys were afraid of dogs, but there was a problem – he did not have enough dogs. Brown contacted a friend in the Turkish Consulate who sent some German shepherds. The dogs were not trained as MWDs, but the enemy didn't know that.

116 top A U.S. Army war dog searches for explosive devices as troops keep a safe distance. IEDs are responsible for more than half of coalition troops – and dogs – killed in action.

116 bottom U.S. Senior Airman Stephen Hanks, 447th Expeditionary Security Forces Squadron Military Working Dog handler, and "Geri," his Patrol and Explosive Detector Dog, look through a window while securing an abandoned building on Dec. 11, 2011 at Sather Air Base in Baghdad, Iraq. Hanks and "Geri" deployed from Patrick Air Force Base, Fla., to provide explosive and psychological deterrence in support of Operation New Dawn.

118-119 U.S. Air Force Sgt. Matthew Templet and "Basco," his Patrol Explosive Detector Dog, search for explosives in an abandoned house in Haji Ghaffar village in the Zari district of Kandahar Province on Dec. 27, 2010. The team deployed from the 627th Security Forces Squadron based at Joint Base Lewis-McChord, Wash.

"They would see these dogs at the checkpoint, just standing there, and the enemy would turn around," Brown said. "Just seeing the dogs walking down the line would cause disruptive people to cease."

While the "deception dogs" brought a smile, the war dogs earned his salute. The general said MWD teams "saved hundreds of my soldiers' lives."

"We used them extensively in every operation we could," he said. "I am confident we are going to see them used in greater measure in years to come. They truly are unsung heroes."

Commanders such as Brown count on dog teams to locate caches that house weapons and ammunition. From June through August 2011, one thousand one hundred and sixty-two caches were found in Afghanistan, an increase of eighty-three percent when compared to the same period in 2010.

Teams also help raid villages when intelligence shows the Taliban is trying to infiltrate or influence the people. Teams also help accompany "time-sensitive target teams" that kick down doors to take down key insurgents. Sometimes the mark is able to slip away and make a run for it, but they never get far.

No matter the mission, battlefield commanders have come to know the critical capability MWDs bring to the fight. Few know this better than Colonel Walter Piatt. The Army's Infantry Commandant has four deployments to Iraq and Afghanistan, including tours as a battalion commander, division operations officer and brigade combat team commander.

"You know what works in combat because soldiers in formations will ask for that," he said. "Military working dogs were always, always the number one request. There was never enough to go around. We can't thank them enough."

The Defense Department has worked to expand this high-demand, low-density asset through a number of programs. Two of the most successful are the Army's Tactical Explosive Detection Dogs and the Marine Corps' IED Detector Dogs.

Both programs started in 2009 and are funded through 2014. They take soldiers and Marines from within a deploying unit — be they cooks, bakers or candlestick makers — and train them for eight weeks to be dog handlers. They are teamed with seasoned SSDs, so no attack or obedience training is necessary. Every battalion then has twelve to twenty dog teams able to sniff out IEDs and other explosives.

Great Britain put a similar program into practice in Afghanistan. The 102 Military Working Dog Squadron took command of the Theatre Military Working Dog Support Unit for Operation Herrick 15, which ran from October 2011 until March 2012. The squadron's eighty military working dogs included a two-fold increase in detection dog capability, and the squadron became the first responsible for commanding specially selected infantry soldiers trained to handle IED detection dogs.

Trained infantrymen are not the only supply source tapped in recent years. Another successful approach has seen hundreds of civilian dog teams hired to provide explosive detection since 2005. As many as seven hundred teams were deployed at the height of operations in Iraq.

This business is worth big bucks, evident by the constant court battles and official protests leveled by contractors trying to land the biggest bite. But when companies such as American K9 and EOD Technology are not fighting each other, they put a serious hurt on enemy operations.

Contract working dog teams are strictly prohibited from offense operations. Most provide explosive detection at control points and key facilities. They typically use the same breeds common to MWD units, and most require handlers have either a military or law enforcement background.

The exact number and type of dog teams in theater at any given moment is anyone's guess. Numerous nations contribute forces and many missions are classified. The variety of the MWD force is evident in Senate testimony by U.S. Army Secretary John McHugh on May 18, 2011. Nearly one thousand dog teams were deployed to both fronts at the time, but only one hundred and eighty-one explosive detection dogs belonged to the Army: seven were in Iraq and the remainder in Afghanistan.

But the influx of these and other explosive detector dog programs have allowed seasoned MWD teams to continue their work alongside special operators in increasingly critical missions.

Military working dog teams do not typically pair with Tier One special operations units such as SEAL Team Six or Delta Force. Those teams have their own dog handlers and their own dog programs, as does the 75th Ranger Regiment. The war dogs of SEAL Team Six became well known in 2011 for the best of reasons ... and the worst. "Cairo," a Belgian Malinois, remains the only named member of the team that located and killed Osama bin Laden on May 1. Three months later, a Belgian Malinois named Bart and his handler, Master at Arms First Class John Douangdara,

were killed when Taliban fighters downed a Chinook helicopter that carried 30 warfighters, including many members of SEAL Team Six. It was the largest single-day loss of life for American forces in Afghanistan.

MWDs are heavily used by other special operations teams such as the Green Berets, other SEAL teams and Marine Special Operations Command. Clandestine ops by commando canines are nothing new. The 2nd Marine Raider Regiment used war dogs during its invasion of Bougainville in World War II. Dog teams were assigned to long-range reconnaissance patrols in May 1964 and SEAL Team Two used two scout dogs, "Rinnie" and "Silver," in Vietnam. "Silver" would later earn jump wings by making five jumps with Quartermaster Third Class Dewayne Schalengerg.

120 U.S. Air Force Senior Airman Stephen Hanks and "Geri," his Patrol and Explosive Detector Dog, check an abandoned building on Sather Air Base in Baghdad, Iraq, for explosives and squatters on Dec. 11, 2011. The team are part of the 447th Expeditionary Security Forces Squadron supporting Operation New Dawn.

121 A thorough scan of buildings and roadways is essential to defeating an ever-evolving enemy. Today, three out of four bombs in Afghanistan use fertilizer-based homemade explosives as the main charge. Dogs, trained to detect military-grade explosives, had to learn to detect very minute portions of explosives such as sugar potassium, ammonium nitrate, potassium chlorate and urea nitrate.

Dog teams assigned to Combined Joint Special Operations Task Force missions know they are at the tip of the spear. These teams do not endure all the inspections, parades and other necessary requirements placed on the conventional Army. They either are in a fight or preparing for the next fight. These teams operate in an indescribably dangerous, difficult and unpredictable environment. Their skills must be honed to razor-sharp perfection and ready to go at a moment's notice.

Whether moving swift and silent or fast and furious, most special operations teams do not use MWDs in an attack role, as many might assume. Instead, the dogs are most often used for explosive detection and added security. As one special operator described it, he

has unparalleled training and technology to help him identify and bring down the bad guy, but needs the dog to find the explosives he cannot see.

The training MWD teams conduct to prepare for these missions would satisfy the most devoted adrenaline junkie. Among them are helocasts, in which the team jumps from a low-flying helicopter into a body of water. Handlers fast rope and rappel out of helicopters so often they could do it while asleep. Handlers also get to SPIE rig – a Special Purpose Insertion/Extraction technique in which soldiers are attached to a rope and lifted out by helicopter. The soldiers are not pulled in, mind you. They get to enjoy the view as they dangle beneath the bird.

122 and 123 Members of Indonesia's elite Armed Forces (Kopasus) along with their specialized war dogs descend from a helicopter during anti-terrorism drills in Jakarta on Oct. 20, 2003.

124-125 U.S. Air Force Staff Sgt. Philip Mendoza pets his Military Working Dog, "Rico" aboard a helicopter.

126-127 U.S. Marines and war dogs from the 2nd Battalion, 8th Marine Regiment of the 2nd Marine Expeditionary Brigade wait for helicopter transport on July 2, 2009. The warriors were part of Operation Khanjar at Camp Dwyer in Helmand Province in Afghanistan.

Of course, special ops training would not be complete without jumping from a perfectly good aircraft. The regular eight hundred-foot mass drops are a good start, but some MWD teams aim much higher.

One is Army Master Sgt. Chris Lalonde and his Belgian Malinois, "Fasco." The duo jumped from 12,500 feet in September 2009. Lalonde said "Fasco," who was secure in an assault vest made by Eagle Industries, was well aware of his surroundings and calmly kept a close eye on other jumpers as they came within proximity.

128-129 and 129 U.S. Army Master Sgt. Chris Lalonde and "Fasco" jump from 12,500 feet above Fort Leonard Wood, Missouri in September 2009. The duo jumped with the 101st Airborne Division Skydiving team. Lalonde is a legend among dog handlers. With two decades of strong service, to include three bronze stars and eight combat deployments, Lalonde is a likely candidate to become the first canine sergeant major in Army history.

130-131 and 131 *After a brief rest on the flight line (left), a Military Working Dog heads to a waiting helicopter on March 7, 2011, during exercise Emerald Warrior at Hurlburt Field, Fla. The two week joint/combined tactical exercise sponsored by U.S. Special Operations Command is designed to leverage lessons learned from operations Iraqi and Enduring Freedom to provide trained and ready forces to combatant commanders.*

132 U.S. Air Force Staff Sgt. Manny Garcia and war dog "Jimmy," both from the 35th Security Forces Squadron, board a helicopter on Feb. 28, 2006 outside of Forward Operations Base Normandy, in Diyala, Iraq. The team had just swept a farm for weapons and items used to make improvised explosive devices.

133 U.S. Navy Master-at-Arms 2nd Class Robert Pennington, with Task Force Military Police (TFMP), 3rd Battalion, 3rd Marine Regiment, sits with his war dog, "Amty," aboard a CH-53E Super Stallion helicopter. The team was taking the troop transport from Al Asad Air Base to Combat Outpost Rawah, Iraq, on June 2, 2009.

134　A U.S. soldier assigned to the 4th Battalion, 10th Special Forces Group prepares to fast rope out of a CH-47 Chinook helicopter near Tallahassee Regional Airport, Fla., on March 2, 2011. The team was participating in Emerald Warrior, an annual two-week joint/combined tactical exercise sponsored by U.S. Special Operations Command to provide realistic training opportunities to conventional and special operations forces.

135 Springer Spaniel Toby, an eight-year-old explosive detection dog, arrives with British forces at Mus Qala in the southern Afghan province of Helmand on March 23, 2006. The British troops were tasked with restoring security to the violent province, where Taliban forces controlled much of the countryside and were financed by protecting the heroin poppy trade.

136-137 Brady Rusk, 12, hugs "Eli" at a retirement and adoption ceremony held Feb. 3, 2011 at Lackland Air Force Base, Texas. The bomb-sniffing Labrador Retriever was assigned to Brady's older brother, Marine Pfc. Colton Rusk, 20, who was killed in action in Afghanistan by Taliban sniper fire Dec. 5.

Sadly, such achievements are not the only memories being made in the War on Terror. Like many heroic soldiers with whom they serve, some war dogs suffer from post-traumatic stress disorder. This reduces a once brave war dog into a timid canine that may never be able to return to duty.

There is no denying that PTSD is a far-reaching reality. It is estimated that twenty percent of Operation Enduring Freedom and Operation Iraqi Freedom veterans have experienced post-traumatic stress disorder. Funding by the Veterans' Administration for intramural PTSD research increased from $9.9 million in fiscal 2005 to $24.5 million in fiscal year 2009.

It is hard to determine why one dog will suffer with PTSD while another does not. Much like the soldiers with whom they serve each are individuals with unique characteristics.

One emerging discussion among handlers is the apparent prevalence of PTSD in the SSD dog community. The Defense Department did not provide data to refute or support the claim, but dozens of handlers said they see the problem most often in SSDs — and they think they know why.

Specialized Search Dogs are not trained to bite. They are trained only to find explosives

137 U.S. Marine Staff Sgt. Dana Brown, battalion kennel master, gives Cpl. Richard Bock a comforting hug during the memorial service in honor of "Keve," a Military Working Dog who died in 2009.

Patrol Explosive Detection Dogs are trained to find explosives and, like SSDs, are rewarded for doing so. But they also are trained to bite and attack on command, which handlers say is a way to get stress and pent-up aggression out. An SSD, on the other hand, deals with the same emotions but does not have a way to get rid of them.

The result, handlers say, is a dog that is more susceptible to PTSD. And as it does with their human counterparts, PTSD affects different war dogs in different ways. Some become clingy and needy, others become distant and timid, and others still will become irritable or aggressive.

A common reaction is hyper vigilance, or an effort to escape or avoid places in which they used to be comfortable. "Gypsy," a PEDD from Fort Belvoir, Virginia, began showing these symptoms in 2011.

She located an explosive device while attached to a special operations unit. As the team took action, an enemy soldier used a command wire to detonate a secondary explosion. "Gypsy" was not seriously injured in the blast, but began to correlate the secondary explosion with her initial find. She seemed to expect a second explosion on subsequent finds, and would walk around the explosive instead of sitting as she was trained to do. The kennel and base vet teamed to help "Gypsy" overcome her fears, and they have experience in this field.

Another PEDD, "Jofa," showed some of the same tendencies after the January 12, 2011 blast that killed his handler, Army Sgt. Zainah Creamer. The team was clearing routes and buildings in Afghanistan's Kandahar Province. Kennel Master Sgt. 1st Class Chad Jones said "Jofa" "just wasn't the same" when he returned. All the handlers pitched in on Creamer's behalf and through some time, training and tenderness, "Jofa" has regained his former capabilities and continues to press on.

Other dogs will show a complete change of behavior. One that was aggressive might become scared of everything. The dog will tuck its tail between its legs and even roll on its back in full submission when approached by a stranger.

A handler will take the dog to the vet the moment he identifies any change in behavior. The vet can recommend any number of things. He can put the dog under observation or on light duty to let the dog just be a dog for a little while. No work is involved, no commands are given. The dog is simply treated to some rest and relaxation. Some dogs are so distressed they require antidepressants or anti-anxiety medication.

A dog that is unable to return to duty will be sent home. If the behavior continues the dog will likely

RANCHO COASTAL HUMANE SOCIETY PRO...
HONORS THE MILITARY WORKING DO...

DEDICATED TO
ALL MILITARY WORKING DOGS
AND THEIR HANDLERS
PAST, PRESENT AND FUTURE.
YOUR DEEDS AND SACRIFICES
WILL ALWAYS BE REMEMBERED.

end up under the care of Dr. Walter Burghardt, chief of behavioral medicine for military working dog studies at the Daniel E. Holland Military Working Dog Hospital at Lackland Air Force Base, Texas.

Burghardt is the Defense Department's only animal behavioral specialist. The veterinarian holds a master's degree in psychology and a doctorate in biopsychology, and has thirty years of experience in this field.

Burghardt and his colleagues treat dozens of cases each year with medication, therapy or a combination of the two. Therapy includes treatments such as desensitization and counter-conditioning. Of every four dogs under his care, one will return to service, one will be reassigned to another job, one will be retired and adopted and one will need prolonged therapy for up to six months.

138-139 The Rancho Coastal Humane Society's Military Working Dog Memorial in Encinitas, Calif., is one of only a handful of memorials honoring war dog service.

25 MARINE WAR DOGS GAVE THEIR
GUAM IN 1944. THEY SERVED AS SENTRIES
THEY EXPLORED CAVES, DETECTED
SEMPER FIDELIS
KURT
YONNIE
SKIPPER
PONCHO
NIG
PRINCE
MISSY
CAPPY
BLITZ
ARNO
BURSCH
PEPPER
TAM
GIVEN IN THEIR MEMORY AND
OF THE 2nd AND 3rd MARINE
OWE THEIR LIVES TO THE
BY WILLIAM W. PUTNEY
DEDICATED

140 Petty Officer 2nd Class Blake Soller pets his Military Working Dog, "Rico," at the War Dog Cemetery located on Naval Base Guam on Oct. 27, 2006.

140-141 A guard dog from the K-9 unit of the Philippine Army rests in the shade along the graves inside the Manila American cemetery in the Philippine capital on May 24, 2009. At least 17,000 graves lay in the memorial park that pays tribute to U.S. and Philippine soldiers that fought side by side during World War II.

Neither the war dogs' heroic contributions on the battlefield, or the physical and emotional scars many survivors carry, are formally recognized by the Defense Department. Without doubt though, war dog heroes are known, nonetheless.

Stubby

"Stubby" is the granddaddy of all hero dogs. He did not have a military pedigree, or military training for that matter. However, this stray Bull Terrier mix earned distinction as the most decorated war dog in U.S. military history.

Private J. Robert Conroy brought "Stubby" along when the 102nd Infantry, 26th (Yankee) Division was called to duty in World War I. The dog, only a few weeks old, was smuggled aboard a transport ship that took the soldiers to France in July 1917.

"Stubby" served nineteen months and participated in seventeen battles to include Chateau Thierry, the Marne and the Meuse-Argonne. In addition, the dog, named for his short tail, proved his worth time and time again.

"Stubby" became very sensitive to the acrid aroma of poison gas after an attack nearly killed him. His painful memory became a lifesaver when the Germans launched an early morning gas attack weeks later. The approaching odor drove an agitated "Stubby" through the trench, barking and biting the sleeping soldiers until they took necessary action.

"Stubby"'s keen sense of smell on another occasion uncovered a German infiltrator making a map of allied positions. The German made a break for it, but was brought down by persistent bites to his lower legs and still "Stubby" did not relent. The dog sunk his teeth into the German's rear-end, and held on until friendly forces arrived.

142-143 Louise Johnson and "Stubby," history's most decorated war dog, participate in a parade on May 15, 1921 in Washington, D.C. "Stubby," who would meet three Presidents, is wearing wound and service stripes earned in action.

The American soldiers quickly recognized the dog's courage and capability and commissioned "Stubby" to locate wounded soldiers in the deadly badlands that lay between bloody trenches. His bark would lead medics to the wounded, and alert them to the presence of an approaching enemy.

Such remarkable achievements came at a cost. The hero dog suffered wounds of his own, which included shrapnel in his chest and right leg from a German grenade. He required several operations at a field hospital before rejoining the Yankee Division.

"Stubby" was with the division when President Woodrow Wilson paid a visit on Christmas Day 1918. It would not be the last president the war dog would meet.

"Stubby" became an American folk hero after the war. He took part in countless parades, war bond rallies and hospital visits. He was given life membership in the American Legion and the Red Cross.

Gen. John "Black Jack" Pershing awarded "Stubby" a Gold Medal in 1921. The canine sergeant paid the White House a visit later that year, where he met President Warren G. Harding. The renowned canine met President Calvin Coolidge three years later.

"Stubby" died on March 16, 1926. His remains are preserved at the Smithsonian Institution, but his selfless service would be seen in hundreds of dogs that served in the World War II.

Chips

Most notable among the World War II canine corps is "Chips," a German Shepherd/Husky mix that was the most decorated war dog of World War II – but for all the wrong reasons.

The two-year-old sentry dog was trained at Front Royal, Virginia in 1942, and was in the middle of some ferocious fighting a short time later. "Chips" first served in then-Maj. Gen. George Patton's North Africa Campaign of 1942. Less than one year later the war dog landed on heavily defended beaches with the 3rd Division of Patton's Seventh Army during the successful invasion of Sicily.

Soon after the invasion, "Chips" and his handler drew near a well-camouflaged pillbox while on patrol. "Chips" became aggressive and broke free. Machinegun fire erupted as the dog raced toward the enemy. The shooting stopped moments later. An Italian soldier, bleeding from bites to his arms and throat, emerged with hands raised. Three soldiers followed behind him.

It was later learned that an Italian had fired a revolver at point-blank range in an effort to stop "Chips," but missed the mark. The relentless dog did not let the scalp wound and powder burns stop him as he single-handedly silenced the would-be ambush.

"Chips" was recommended in September 1943 for the Distinguished Service Cross, a heroism award second only to the Medal of Honor. The commanding general knocked it down to a Silver Star, prestigious in its own right. "Chips" also received a Purple Heart for combat wounds, and the personal thanks of Gen. Dwight D. Eisenhower.

However, William Thomas, the 1943 national commander of the Military Order of the Purple Heart protested. In letters to President Franklin D. Roosevelt and the War Department, Thomas asserted that giving a dog an award designed for a soldier "decries the high and lofty purpose for which the medal was created." He went on to say, that dogs should have their own medal designed, but that aspect of his letter was lost to history.

The result was a new policy that remains in effect today: U.S. military decorations were for humans only. Countless handlers have ignored the rule and "shared" their medals with their partner. Some commands go as far as to approve service awards for working dogs. Nevertheless, this policy continues to be a point of contention for handlers whose dogs serve – and die – on the front lines.

---

145 "Chips" gets a donut from a fellow soldier in 1944. The German Shepherd/Husky mix was recommended in September 1943 for the Distinguished Service Cross, an heroism award second only to the Medal of Honor. The Commanding General knocked it down to a Silver Star. "Chips" also received a Purple Heart for combat wounds, and the personal thanks of Gen. Dwight D. Eisenhower.

York, Budda and Nemo

On the other hand, there are war dogs that are so good that everyone goes home alive.

One such dog was "York." The scout dog led 148 patrols with the 26th Infantry Scout Dog Platoon in Korea from June 12, 1951 to June 26, 1953. Not one man was killed when "York" was part of the patrol. Gen. Samuel T. Williams was so impressed he awarded the "York" the Distinguished Service Award for his service.

York remained in the Far East until 1957, when he returned to the United States to help with recruiting and public relations. After a short stint at Fort Carson, Colorado, "York" was transferred to Fort Benning, Georgia. There, he was once again attached to the 26th Infantry Scout Dog Platoon – the same unit with which he served in Korea.

"Budda" had similar success in Vietnam. The dog served five years – longer than any other scout dog in Vietnam. He had five confirmed enemy kills in close combat and was wounded three times, including a

spear in the neck from a punji pit. He had eight handlers, all of whom returned home.

While "Budda"'s notoriety is based on longevity, a sentry dog named "Nemo" made his mark in a single act of selfless service.

Other dogs put their own lives on the line in an effort to protect their handler. A2C Robert Thorneburg was hit on December 4, 1966 when enemy sappers infiltrated the Tan Son Nhut airbase in South Vietnam. "Nemo" immediately attacked and took down two aggressors. The dog was shot in the face; the round hit him in his right eye and exited through his mouth. Still, the wounded dog crawled across Thorneburg in an effort to protect his master.

Veterinarian Capt. Raymond Huston conducted skin grafts on "Nemo"'s face, performed a tracheotomy and removed the dog's right eye. The skilled vet was successful in saving the dog's life, but "Nemo" on June 23, 1967 became the first sentry

146 *Airmen and veterinarians treat "Nemo" in June 1967 after he attacked enemy sappers at Tan Son Nhut airbase in South Vietnam. The war dog, shot in the face, required a tracheotomy and lost his right eye.*

dog to be retired from active duty in Vietnam. He became a canine recruiter before dying on March 15, 1973.

A similar sapper infiltration nearly two years later would result in the only Medal of Honor to date to be awarded to a working dog handler.

Carlo

The old threat of chemical warfare, not encountered since World War I, returned in Operations Desert Shield and Desert Storm. Dog teams were issued atropine auto-injectors as a precaution.

Thankfully, the chemical threat never materialized. But the threat of explosives proved all too real.

"Carlo" and his handler, Air Force Staff Sgt. Christopher Batta, were called on to eliminate that threat. The team made a lasting impact during the 60 days they served in Kuwait. The dog alerted to one hundred and sixty-seven explosives and caches. One booby-trap uncovered was made of cluster bombs

and hidden beneath a case of Meals, Ready-to-Eat.

When Batta was awarded the Bronze Star, the handler removed his medal and placed it on his partner saying "'Carlo' worked harder than me. He was always in front of me."

"Carlo" and Batta were not the only team to work hard. The unprecedented flood of war prisoners proved problematic when Kuwait was liberated in late February 1991. Thousands of Iraqi soldiers were captured or surrendered. Royal Air Force Police dog handlers were sent to Mary Hill Camp, a compound that housed roughly four thousand prisoners. It was not uncommon for one dog team to control four hundred prisoners at a time – yet not one prisoner was lost.

Dog teams have been deployed with regularity in the years that followed. They helped take down drug lords and terrorists. They provided security as well as search and rescue.

147 *U.S. Air Force Tech. Sgt. Rudy Muccitilli (right) and Sgt. Chris Batta search with their dog "Carlo" for weapons and bombs in Iraqi bunkers North of Kuwait City on March 10, 1991. The team in 60 days found 167 explosives and caches.*

Lex

"Lex" was an eight-year-old German Shepherd serving in Fallujah, Iraq. His patrol on March 21, 2007, came under heavy attack. A mortar claimed the life of his handler, 20-year-old Marine Cpl. Dustin Lee.

"Lex," critically injured in the attack, refused to leave his partner's side. Today, he stands beside Lee's family as they fight the painful battle known by every family to have lost a loved one on the field of battle.

With the help of Rep. Walter B. Jones (R-N.C.), "Lex" was granted early retirement and was presented to Lee's family on Dec. 21, 2007.

"It's not going to bring back my brother, but it's something close to it," said Dustin's 16-year-old sister, Madison, as she played with "Lex."

The action inspired Jones to write the "Corporal Dustin Lee Memorial Act," which would allow military working dogs to be retired early and pre-

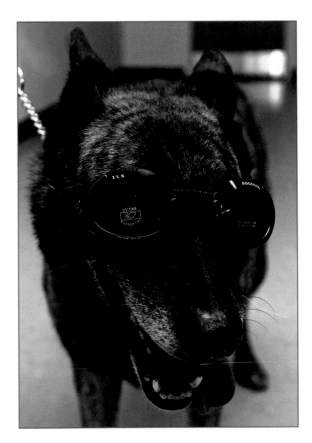

sented to grieving families or handlers so seriously wounded that they require medical discharge.

One such adoption was granted on February 3, 2011, to the family of Marine Pfc. Colton Rusk. One letter the 20-year-old Marine sent home had a smudge with the words "Eli's kisses" written beneath. When Rusk was killed by sniper fire on December 5, 2010, in Helmand province, Afghanistan, "Eli" instinctively crawled atop his fallen handler. When presented to the family, the black Labrador Retriever first kissed Rusk's mother then fell into the arms of Rusk's father.

"Lex," who bravely ventured into uncharted territories as a military working dog, made a similar journey four years after his adoption. But "Lex" was not looking for bombs this time. He was looking for a revolutionary stem cell treatment to help him overcome wounds he received in the attack that claimed his handler's life.

Shrapnel lodged in "Lex"'s spine caused debilitating back and joint pain and prevented him from walking on his own. "Lex" received a three-day stem cell treatment that helped him grow new cartilage. Stem cells from his own fat were injected into the affected joint. He fully recovered within two months, and his success has paved the way for many other dogs who suffer with similar ailments.

Bino

Other dogs have become heroes after returning home. "Bino" is such a dog. The Dutch Shepherd served with the U.S. Army in Tikrit and Mosul, Iraq. The retired narcotics detector was adopted by Debbie Kandoll, founder of Military Working Dog Adoptions. He now helps train retired war dogs to serve veterans who suffer with Post Traumatic Stress Disorder and Traumatic Brain Injury.

148 "Bino" sports a pair of dog goggles that he wore on patrol in the Iraqi desert.

149 Camryn Lee and "Lex" share a little affection. The Lee family adopted the German Shepherd. The adoption marked the first time the U.S. military has granted early retirement to a working dog so it could live with a former handler's family.

And he is not alone. Groups such as Veterans Moving Forward and Dog Bless You are turning to service and retired military working dogs to help veterans as they battle back from their injuries. The latter agency vowed to donate a service dog to a recent veteran for every five thousand "likes" the Dog Bless You Facebook page gets, up to one hundred dogs. The page had more than two hundred and seventy five thousand "likes" by mid-November 2011.

The 13-year-old "Bino" earned a 2011 American Humane Association Hero Dog Award for his military service and continuing contributions to American society.

Buster, Sadie and Treo

While the United States military lacks a formal award program to honor hero dogs, the Brits recognize their best with the People's Dispensary for Sick Animals Dickin Medal — the animal equivalent of the Victoria Cross.

Three dogs have received the award for their contributions in the War on Terror.

The first was "Buster," a Springer Spaniel who served in March 2003 with the Duke of Wellington's Regiment in Safwan, Iraq. British troops were getting hammered by rocket attacks. Intelligence pointed to an extremist group as the culprit, but three searches failed to turn up any evidence. Then "Buster" was called in. He found a cache hidden behind a false wall. It contained AK47 assault rifles, suitcases full of cash, grenades, ammunition and bomb-making equipment. The bad guys were caught, the attacks stopped and lives were saved.

It would be more than three years before another Dickin Medal would be awarded. This time it was "Sadie," a Labrador assigned to the Royal Gloucestershire, Berkshire and Wiltshire Regiment.

The veteran of Iraq and Bosnia in November 2005 located a bomb planted at the United Nations headquarters in Kabul, Afghanistan.

150 "Buster," a 5-year-old Springer Spaniel attached to the Royal Army Veterinary Corps, is awarded the People's Dispensary for Sick Animals Dickin Medal on December 9, 2003 in London. Sharing this honor, known as "the animal's Victoria Cross," is "Buster"'s handler Sgt. Danny Morgan. "Buster" helped save the lives of troops and civilians earlier this year in southern Iraq when he located a hidden cache of arms, explosives and bomb-making equipment.

The find came moments after a suicide bomb ripped through the area. "Sadie" went to work amid the chaos and carnage and picked up the scent of a second device through two feet of concrete. The remote-controlled bomb, which was a pressure cooker, filled with TNT and covered with sandbags. It was designed to kill rescue workers responding to the suicide attack.

"Sadie"'s handler, Lance Cpl. Karen Yardley, shouted warnings that quickly cleared the area as a bomb disposal team moved in.

"Treo," an eight-year-old black Labrador, became the third dog of the modern era to receive the coveted award on February 24, 2010.

The explosive detector and his handler, Sgt. Dave Heyhoe, deployed in 2008 as part of 104 Military Working Dogs Support Unit attached to a platoon from the 1st Battalion Royal Irish Regiment near Sangin, Afghanistan. "Treo" was credited with saving untold lives when he alerted to booby traps and improvised explosive devices on two patrols.

Maj. Graham Shannon, commander of the 1st Battalion Royal Irish Regiment, said "Treo's nose kept my soldiers safe from the roadside bombs planted by the Taliban to maximize injuries and deaths among troops. The Military Working Dogs play a vital role in our patrols detecting these devices and the dogs themselves show enormous amounts of courage doing this work every day, and on many occasions, under attack. "It is fitting that 'Treo' has been recognized for the protection he afforded the troops through the presentation of this award."

"Treo" retired in August 2009 and was adopted by Heyhoe and his family.

Despite the high honors, "Buster," "Sadie" and "Treo" are not the most famous war dogs to emerge from the War on Terror. That distinction belongs to "Cairo," a German Shepherd that accompanied SEAL Team Six on the mission that killed Osama bin Laden. In fact, "Cairo" is the only member of the team whose name is known to the public.

151 "Treo," an eight-year-old black Labrador, on Feb. 24, 2010 became the third war dog of the modern era to be presented Britain's Dickin medal, awarded for bravery and commitment in wartime, the highest military honor an animal can expect. Here, "Treo" poses with the medal at the Imperial War Museum in London. "Treo" was decorated for his work sniffing out explosives in Afghanistan.

Cairo

The mission was first detailed in "Getting Bin Laden: What happened that night in Abbottabad," an August 8, 2011 article penned by Nicholas Schmidle for New Yorker magazine. Schmidle used firsthand reports from team members and spec ops commanders and controllers.

The Belgian Malinois was aboard Helo Two. "Cairo" was strapped to an assault team member as the team neared its target and "fast roped" out of a secret, stealth Black Hawk helicopter in the dark of night.

"Cairo" took position on the one-acre compound's northeast side. The insertion had been rehearsed dozens of times at replica compounds in North Carolina and Nevada in the weeks prior. "Cairo" flew on every practice run that mimicked the flight from Jalalabad to Abbottabad, which is about a hundred and twenty miles across the Pakistan border.

The veteran war dog remained quiet as he provided perimeter security in the middle-class neighborhood. Cairo was trusted to locate bin Laden if the terrorist leader had a safe room hidden behind false walls, but his skill was not needed. The faint whisp of suppressed Sig Sauer P226 pistols, Colt M4 rifles and Heckler & Koch MP7s that filled the three-story house soon fell silent when 5.56mm bullets struck bin Laden first in the chest then above his left eye.

The shooters report soon followed over the radio: "For God and country — Geronimo, Geronimo, Geronimo," which was the team's code name for bin Laden.

152 A Military Working Dog outfitted with specialized gear is seen in this undated handout image released by the Canadian company "K9 Storm Inc." which manufactures specialized gear such as high-tech canine flak jackets and tactical body armor used by the U.S. military and other nations. "Cairo," the war dog that accompanied Navy SEAL Team Six commandos in the raid that killed Osama bin Laden, was likely wearing gear similar to this.

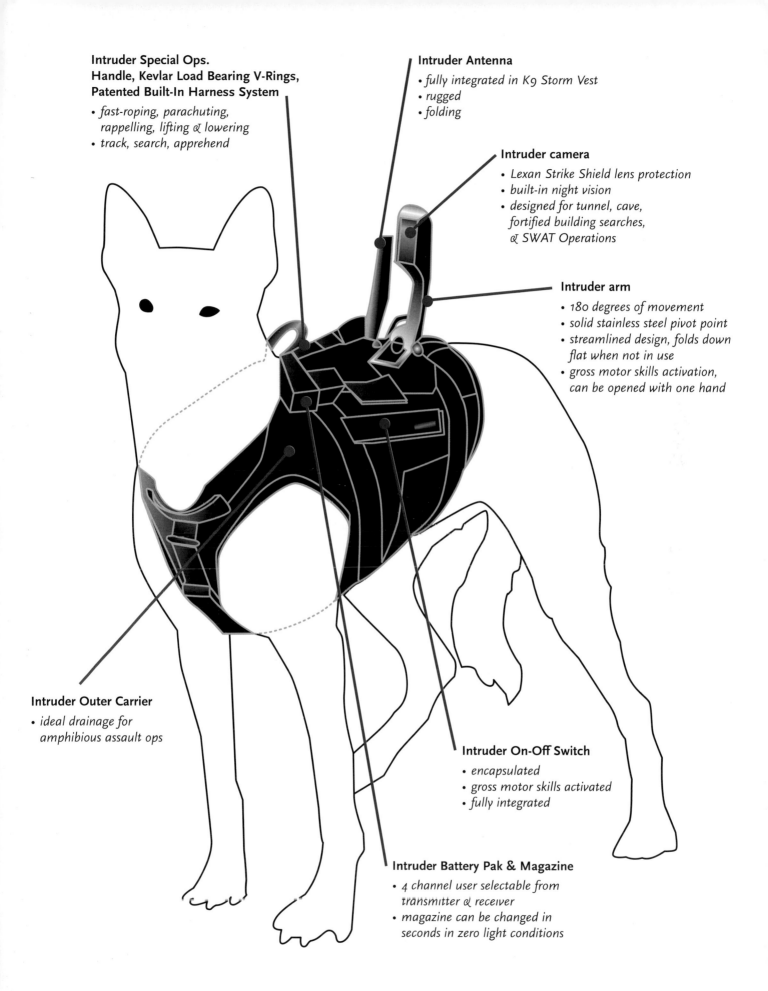

**Intruder Special Ops.
Handle, Kevlar Load Bearing V-Rings,
Patented Built-In Harness System**

• *fast-roping, parachuting,
  rappelling, lifting & lowering*
• *track, search, apprehend*

Intruder Antenna

• *fully integrated in K9 Storm Vest*
• *rugged*
• *folding*

Intruder camera

• *Lexan Strike Shield lens protection*
• *built-in night vision*
• *designed for tunnel, cave,
  fortified building searches,
  & SWAT Operations*

Intruder arm

• *180 degrees of movement*
• *solid stainless steel pivot point*
• *streamlined design, folds down
  flat when not in use*
• *gross motor skills activation,
  can be opened with one hand*

Intruder Outer Carrier

• *ideal drainage for
  amphibious assault ops*

Intruder On-Off Switch

• *encapsulated*
• *gross motor skills activated*
• *fully integrated*

Intruder Battery Pak & Magazine

• *4 channel user selectable from
  transmitter & receiver*
• *magazine can be changed in
  seconds in zero light conditions*

154-155 A Military Working Dog outfitted with its own equipment and light searches a building in zero light conditions. The K9 Storm Intruder is a piece of gear that provides real-time video feed back through multiple fortified barriers. Night vision capabilities adjust automatically to various light conditions for optimal high resolution video.

155 Special Operations forces increasingly rely on war dogs in clandestine and covert missions.
The dogs adapt well to the fast-paced environment, and provide a level of human and explosive
detection that the most advanced technologies cannot replicate.

156-157 *President Obama watches the mission unfold at the White House along with (left) Vice President Joe Biden, (right) Defence Secretary Robert Gates, and (second right) Secretary of State Hillary Clinton, alongside other Security staff, including (back left) Chairman of the Joint Chiefs Admiral Mike Mullen, (back without a tie) National Security Adviser Tom Donilon and (back right, white shirt) Counter-Terrorism chief John Brennan.*

President Barak Obama was unaware that a war dog had participated in the mission when he met SEAL Team 6 a short time later. At the president's request, a muzzled "Cairo" was brought in to meet the commander in chief.

Obama then presented the team a Presidential Unit Citation and said, "Our intelligence professionals did some amazing work. I had fifty-fifty confidence that bin Laden was there, but I had one-hundred-per-cent confidence in you guys. You are, literally, the finest small-fighting force that has ever existed in the world."

The team then presented Obama an American three-by-five flag that had been on board one of the helicopters. The SEALs and pilots signed the back of the flag. An inscription on the front read, "From the Joint Task Force Operation Neptune's Spear, 01 May 2011: 'For God and country. Geronimo.'"

"Cairo" awakened the world to the heroic service provided by war dogs. It is a recognition for which many have fought for years.

Some, such as Rep. Jones, fight their battles on the political front. In addition to the Corporal Dustin Lee Memorial Act, the North Carolina congressman has introduced legislation that would elevate working dogs from the status of military equipment to better honor their worth and contribution.

157 *This is Osama bin Laden's compound in Abbottabad, Pakistan. Navy SEAL Team Six and war dog Cairo, a Belgian Malinois, conducted a daring night raid here on May 1, 2011, killing the al Qaida leader.*

AUTHORS

RONALD L. AIELLO *served in the United States Marine Corps from 1964 to 1970. During this period Ron had the honor of serving with the First Marine Scout Dog Platoon.*
He and his dog "Stormy" were one of the first thirty Marine Scout Dog Teams to be deployed to Vietnam in early 1966. Ron and "Stormy" were involved in many operations leading Marine units in search and destroy missions. Due to Ron's unique perspective he has been a consultant for numerous film producers, screenwriters, book authors, national and local newspapers and has done many TV and Radio interviews. His expertise in the world of training and Military Working Dogs places him in high demand. He's president of the United States War Dogs Association.

LANCE M. BACON *covers leadership, weaponry, training and tactics as senior writer for "Army Times". His combat coverage in Afghanistan includes an award-winning piece on the Battle of Roberts Ridge. Bacon previously served as managing editor of "Air Force Times" and the Kinston (N.C.) "Free Press", a paper twice honored as best in the state and recipient of the Freedom of Excellence Award and the Associated Press' Openness in Government Award. Bacon is a Marine veteran who spent two years aboard USS Independence (CV-62), two years with 2nd Light Armored Reconnaissance Battalion in Camp Lejeune, N.C., and four years in Public Affairs where he was twice recognized as the Marine Corps' journalist of the year.*

BIBLIOGRAPHY

History

- Michael Lemish, "Forever Forward: K-9 Operations in Vietnam" (Schiffer Military History, 2009)
- Michael Lemish, "War Dogs: A History of Loyalty and Heroism" (Potomac Books, Inc., 1999)
- William W. Putney, "Always Faithful: A Memoir of the Marine Dogs of WWII" (Free Press, 2001)
- Nigel Allsopp, "Cry Havoc: The History of War Dogs" (New Holland Publishers, Australia, 2011)

Chapter 1

- Michael L. Hammerstrom, "Ground Dog Day: Lessons Don't Have to be Relearned in the Use of Dogs in Combat" (M.A. Thesis, Naval Post Graduate School, December 2005)
- LCDR Mary Kathleen Murray, USN, "The Contributions of the American Military Working Dog in Vietnam" (M.A. thesis, U.S. Army Command and General Staff College, 1998)
- Department of the Army, Army Concept Team in Vietnam, "60th Infantry Platoon (Scout Dog) Mine/Tunnel Detector Dog" January 1970

Chapter 2

- USA Today "Dogs take a lead in Iraq's terror war" (March 23, 2010)
- Army Regulation 190–12, "Military Police: Military Working Dog Program."
- Alabama A&M and Auburn universities, "The Dog's Sense of Smell" (June 2011)
- Stewart Hilliard, PhD, "The Deferred Final Response Method for Training Substance Detection Dogs: Trouble-Shooting the Final Response" (Military Working Dog Course)

Chapter 3

- The Army Medical Department Journal, "Overview of Combat Trauma in Military Working Dogs in Iraq and Afghanistan," (Jan-March 2009)

- Los Angeles Times, "Afghanistan's most loyal troops" (February 08, 2011)
- USA Today, "At grim milestone for U.S. deaths in Iraq war, a time to reflect" (Dec. 31, 2006)
- Associated Press, "UK Soldier, Dog on Final Mission Together" (March 10, 2011)
- US Fed News, "Guantanamo Bay's K-9 war hero retires from active duty" (October 27, 2011)
- Joint Improvised Explosive Device Defeat Organization, "Statistical Report: IED by Month" (September 2011)
- Linda Crippen, "Military Working Dogs: Guardians of the Night" (Army Training and Doctrine Command, May 23, 2011)
- Department of Defense Directive 5200.31E, August 10, 2011
- States News Service, "Working dogs are man's best friend in Afghanistan" (October 21, 2011)
- Nicholas Schmidle, "Getting Bin Laden: What happened that night in Abbottabad" (The New Yorker, Aug. 8, 2011)
- Michelle Tan, "Dogs bring home war's stress, too" (Air Force Times, December 27, 2010)

Chapter 4

- Lackland AFB, AETC "The Quiet Americans: A History of Military Working Dogs" (2000).
- Associated Press, "Family adopts slain son's military dog" (Dec. 21, 2007)
- Defense Media Activity-San Antonio, "Fallen Marine's family adopts his best friend" (February 3, 2011)
- State News Service "UK Government: A pedigree chum receives highest animal honour" (February 24, 2010)
- Nicholas Schmidle, "Getting Bin Laden: What happened that night in Abbottabad" (The New Yorker, Aug. 8, 2011)

PHOTO CREDITS

AP Photo/LaPresse: *pages 32-33, 34-35, 36, 42-43, 44-45, 46-47*

AP Photo/National Archives via the National World War II
Museum/LaPresse: *page 37*

Archivio White Star: *page 153*

Augusta Chronicle/ZUMAPRESS.com: *page 148*

Bain News Service/Buyenlarge/Getty Images: *pages 20-21*

Patrick Baz/AFP/Getty Images: *pages 108-109*

Bettmann/Corbis: *pages 22-23, 142-143, 145*

Harriet Chalmers Adams/National Geographic Society/Corbis:
pages 16-17

China Daily/Reuters/Contrasto: *pages 54, 54-55*

Andrea Comas/Reuters/Contrasto: *pages 96, 100-101*

Corbis: *page 33*

Bryan Denton/Corbis: *page 67*

Marco Di Lauro/Getty Images: *pages 70, 88-89*

R. A. Elder/Hulton Archive/Getty Images: *pages 40-41*

Vasily Fedosenko/Reuters/Contrasto: *pages 52, 53*

Terry Fincher/Getty Images: *pages 8-9*

David Furst/AFP/Getty Images: *page 88*

Romeo Gacad/AFP/Getty Images: *pages 96-97*

Johann Hattingh/Beeld/zReportage.com/ZUMApress.com: *pages 94-95,
95, 101, 116 top, 121*

Haynes Archive/Popperfoto/Getty Images: *page 26*

Kate Holt/eyevine/Contrasto: *pages 112-113*

Chris Hondros/Getty Images: *pages 114-115*

Massoud Hossaini/AFP/Getty Images: *pages 98-99, 99*

Hulton-Deutsch Collection/Corbis: *pages 25, 28-29*

Bay Ismoyo/AFP/Getty Images: *pages 86-87, 123*

Dmitry Kostyukov/AFP/Getty Images: *pages 14-15*

David Longstreath/AP Photo/LaPresse: *page 147*

Behrouz Mehri/AFP/Getty Images: *pages 12-13, 110-111, 111, 118-119*

John Moore/Getty Images: *page 135*

Nick Morris/Southcreek Global/ZUMApress.com: *pages 72-73*

Ho New/Reuters/Contrasto: *pages 154-155*

Jose Nicolas/Sygma/Corbis: *pages 50-51, 51*

Walter Petruska/AP Photo/LaPresse: *page 149*

David Pollack/K.J. Historical/Corbis: *page 3*

Popperfoto/Getty Images: *pages 18-19, 24, 26-27*

Jaime Rius/AFP/Getty Images: *pages 140-141*

Manpreet Romana/AFP/Getty Images: *pages 126-127*

Torsten Silz/AFP/Getty Images: *page 49*

Christophe Simon/AFP/Getty Images: *pages 91, 92-93*

W. Eugene Smith/Time & Life Pictures/Getty Images: *pages 30-31*

Pete Souza/The White House/ZUMAPRESS.com: *pages 156-157*

Sang Tan/AP Photo/LaPresse: *page 151*

The San Diego Union-Tribune/ZUMAPRESS.com: *pages 138-139*

Dadang Tri/Reuters/Contrasto: *page 122*

Ian Waldie/Getty Images: *page 150*

Andrea Bruce Woodall/The Washington Post/Getty Images: *pages 90-91*

Yslb Pak/Xinhua/ZUMAPRESS.com: *page 157*

Courtesy of Ron Aiello: *pages 11, 38-39, 146*

Courtesy of DefenceImagery.mil: *pages 4-5, 6-7, 57, 58-59, 61, 62, 63, 64,
65, 68, 68-69, 71, 73, 74, 74-75, 76-77, 78, 79 top, 79 bottom, 80-81, 83,
85, 102, 104, 105, 106-107, 116 bottom, 120, 124-125, 128-129, 129, 130-131,
131, 132, 133, 134, 136-137, 137, 140, 160*

Courtesy of K9 Storm Inc.: *pages 152, 155*

Cover – top:

A Belgian Malinois wearing a high-tech combat jacket.
© K9 Storm Inc.

Bottom from left to right:

Dog and trainer exercise as a pair. © DefenceImagery.mil

A historic image from the Second World War battlefields. © Ron Aiello

The spectacular leap from a combat helicopter. © DefenceImagery.mil

The task of searching for explosives is as dangerous as it is
fundamental. © DefenceImagery.mil

ACKNOWLEDGEMENTS

Ronald L. Aiello would like to thank

*His beloved wife Judy and his sons Travis and Nicholas for their
continued support, encouragement and patients in allowing him
to be the person he is today.*

*His good friend John C. Barman (President, JBMF, Inc.) for his
unwavering support over the years.*

*The men, women and their canines who have served and are serving
in the Armed Forces of America for their service and their support
and friendship over the years.*

The Publisher would like to thank

*Defense Imagery Management Operations Center (DIMOC)
(defenseimagery.mil)*

1st Military Working Dog Regiment, The British Army

Debbie Kandoll - MilitaryWorkingDogAdoptions.com

Bill Cummings-The Nemo Committee

K9 Storm Inc.

WHITE STAR PUBLISHERS

WS White Star Publishers® is a registered trademark
property of De Agostini Libri S.p.A.

© 2013 De Agostini Libri S.p.A.
Via G. da Verrazano, 15
28100 Novara, Italy
www.whitestar.it - www.deagostini.it

Editing: Karen O'Brien

ISBN 978-88-544-0657-5
2 3 4 5 6   17 16 15 14 13

Printed in China